Value, Respect, and Attachment

Joseph Raz is one of the world's leading philosophers of law, and in
his Seeley Lectures he reflects critically on one of the central tenets
of ethical thought, the view that values are universal. How can the
latter be so, when evaluative properties are historically or socially
dependent? Professor Raz concludes that we should try to
understand what is and what is not entailed by the universality of
values, with such a proper understanding central to the future
hopes of mankind, rather than abandoning the belief altogether.
This is a concise, pithy, and attractively humane account of some
fundamental questions of social existence, enlivened by examples
drawn from a wide range of sources, including *The Little Prince* of
Saint-Exupéry. It will appeal to students and practitioners of law,
philosophy, and politics.

JOSEPH RAZ is Professor of the Philosophy of Law and a Fellow
of Balliol College, Oxford. He is also Visiting Professor at Columbia
University. A Fellow of the British Academy and an Honorary
Member of the American Academy of Arts and Sciences, Professor
Raz is the author of *The Concept of a Legal System* (Oxford, 1970),
Practical Reason and Norms (Oxford, 1975), *The Authority of Law*
(Oxford, 1979), *The Morality of Freedom* (Oxford, 1986), *Ethics in
the Public Domain* (Oxford, 1994), and *Engaging Reason* (Oxford,
2000).

The John Robert Seeley Lectures have been established by the University of Cambridge as a biennial lecture series in social and political studies, sponsored jointly by the Faculty of History and the University Press. The Seeley Lectures provide a unique forum for distinguished scholars of international reputation to address, in an accessible manner, themes of broad and topical interest in social and political studies. Subsequent to their public delivery in Cambridge the University Press publishes suitably modified versions of each set of lectures. Professor James Tully delivered the inaugural series of Seeley Lectures in 1994 on the theme of *Constitutionalism in an Age of Diversity*.

The Seeley Lectures include

(1) Strange Multiplicity: Constitutionalism in an Age of Diversity
JAMES TULLY
ISBN 0 521 47117 6 (hardback) 0 521 47694 1 (paperback)

(2) The Dignity of Legislation
JEREMY WALDRON
ISBN 0 521 65092 5 (hardback) 0 521 65883 7 (paperback)

(3) Woman and Human Development: The Capabilities Approach
MARTHA NUSSBAUM
ISBN 0 521 66086 6 (hardback) 0 521 003857 (paperback)

(4) Value, Respect, and Attachment
JOSEPH RAZ
ISBN 0 521 80180 X (hardback) 0 521 00022 X (paperback)

VALUE, RESPECT,
AND ATTACHMENT

JOSEPH RAZ

CAMBRIDGE
UNIVERSITY PRESS

PUBLISHED BY THE PRESS SYNDICATE OF THE UNIVERSITY OF CAMBRIDGE
The Pitt Building, Trumpington Street, Cambridge, United Kingdom

CAMBRIDGE UNIVERSITY PRESS
The Edinburgh Building, Cambridge CB2 2RU, UK
40 West 20th Street, New York, NY 10011-4211, USA
10 Stamford Road, Oakleigh, VIC 3166, Australia
Ruiz de Alarcón 13, 28014 Madrid, Spain
Dock House, The Waterfront, Cape Town 8001, South Africa

http://www.cambridge.org

First published 2001

Printed in the United Kingdom at the University Press, Cambridge

Typeface Minion 11/15 pt.   *System* LaTeX 2ε   [TB]

A catalogue record for this book is available from the British Library.

Library of Congress Cataloguing in Publication data

Raz, Joseph.
Value, respect, and attachment / Joseph Raz.
       p.   cm.
Includes bibliographical references and index.
ISBN 0 521 80180 X – ISBN 0 521 00022 X (pb. : alk. paper)
1. Ethics.   2. Values.   I. Title.
BJ1012 .R35   2001
170′.42 – dc21   2001025690

ISBN 0 521 80180 x hardback
ISBN 0 521 00022 x paperback

CONTENTS

vii

Introduction

There is not much in ethical theory which is not widely disputed. One view which enjoys wide support is that values are universal. Nevertheless, it appeared to me that there are uncertainties regarding the meaning and scope of that view which could benefit from further reflection. When invited to give the Seeley lectures of 2000 I decided to use the occasion for yet another, partial and incomplete, reflection on some of the contours of the view that values are universal. I wanted to understand better the significance of this view, and its limits. In particular, I wanted to improve my understanding of how it is compatible with the thought, controverted by many, but compelling to me, that evaluative properties, that is, properties which in themselves make their possessors better or worse, are historically or socially dependent. Social practices are contingent, and changes in them are contingent. If the evaluative depends on the contingent can it be universal? This seemed an appropriate theme for a series of lectures dedicated to the memory of a historian interested in theory and in philosophy, who brought theory to the study of politics and history at Cambridge.

I am aware more of what I did not manage to discuss, or discussed all too briefly and dogmatically, than of what the following pages accomplish. They are very one-sided and partial. Their focus is the tension between partiality and impartiality. Universality seems to imply impartiality. This follows, or seems to follow, once one allows that reasons for action track value.

That is, that the only reason for any action is that the action, in itself or in its consequences, has good-making properties, has features which make it, *pro tanto*, good. I will not discuss this assumption here. But I will accept it, and rely on it. It may seem to follow that since whatever is good is (or derives from what is) good everywhere and at all times (for what does the universality of value mean if it does not entail that?) in pursuing value we are all sharing the same goal, we are all united in the same pursuit. Value is the great uniter, the common bond of mankind. Only mistakes, about what is of value, and about other matters which affect decisions about how to pursue what is of value, can cause discord.

This is a familiar vision, a vision which dominated different cultures from time to time. In the West it fuelled the spirit of optimism bred by the enlightenment whose power we still, sometimes, feel. But only sometimes. Our own perspective is darker and more pessimistic. How can it be otherwise now, as we emerge from the darkest century of human history?

Is belief in the universality of value mistaken? Yes and no. As often understood it is mistaken. But there is a sound core to it. We should understand what is and what is not entailed by the universality of values, rather than abandon that belief altogether. For example, it does not entail that values cannot change over time.[1] Chapter 2 below deals with the illusions and the reality of the universality of value. It may leave the impression that what truth there is in it is technical, that the hope that

---

[1] I have argued for that in chapter 7 of *Engaging Reason* (Oxford: Oxford University Press, 2000). That book contains much of the philosophical background necessarily missing in the reflections which follow here.

the universality of value can be the common bond of mankind is abandoned. But that is not so. Belief in the universality of value is vital for a hopeful perspective for the future. Yet, it is a perspective which allows for diversity within that universality. There is hope there too. To the extent that hope for the future depends on philosophical enlightenment it depends in no small measure on understanding the limits of universality, and the sources and nature of diversity. It depends on reconciling belief in the universality with a correct understanding of the real diversity of values.

Diversity, I will suggest in these pages, arises out of partiality. In the last resort partiality, that is, the favouring of one person or one activity or cause over others, is what lies at the root of legitimate diversity (as well as at the root of much abuse of values for evil aims). The thought is simple. Diversity in evaluative beliefs and practices results either from mistaken beliefs in what is valuable (in which case it is – generally speaking – not legitimate diversity) or from the partiality of people to some people or goals which are all valuable, but to which some people are attracted and committed, whereas others are indifferent, or much less attracted. Given that everyone is partial to something which is genuinely of value, the universality of value is respected. Legitimate diversity results not from the fact that some things are of value to some but not to others, but from the fact that we are differentially attracted to the same values, or to people and goals which are attractive because they possess the same values. Legitimate differential attraction tends to lead to speciation of values aided by the emergence of variant practices exemplifying but at the same time modifying the more abstract values which bred them.

This is bound to sound a mysterious process. But even if partiality can reconcile the diversity of evaluative practices with the universality of value, one may retain one's doubts. Is not partiality itself suspect? Is it not the case that partiality in itself is incompatible with the universality of value? There are several aspects to the problem. One is that when our partiality takes the form of a special attachment to people, places, or other objects it is often accompanied by, and justified by, claims about the uniqueness of the objects of our attachments. But is the unique value of some people or objects consistent with the universality of value? Chapter 1 takes up this theme, exploring it with help from *The Little Prince*.

The second problem is that the logic of deriving reasons from the value of different options points towards a maximising conception of practical reason, which in turn seems to force one to decide between universality and partiality. Let me explain. Most forms of legitimate partiality are more or less optional. We may be required to favour our children or friends, but it is up to us whether to have children or friends. We may have to be partial to our country, or city, but we may emigrate to another country, or choose where to live, and so on. Even more clearly, we may choose whether to devote much time and resources to music or to golf, etc. In all such cases we assume that our choice is free from maximising constraints. That is, we assume that in making these choices we are not required to, perhaps even that we may not, engage in the sort of calculation which should determine the route of a proposed new road, where utilitarian calculations of maximising the expected utility of the road are in place. If partiality involves the legitimacy of choices which are not governed by maximising reasoning, then does it not follow that partiality is inconsistent either with the universality of value or with the value–reason nexus, since it appears that the combination of the two forces maximising logic on all decisions and denies the legitimacy of options which are not subject to it?

In previous writings I argued that the fact that valuable options are often incommensurate leaves plenty of room for partiality. I have not resiled from that belief. My arguments for it have been, beyond doubt, very incomplete, and this is not the place to make good their deficiencies. One major lacuna in the picture, however, is taken up here. I have argued that given how pervasive are cases of reasons for alternative options being incommensurate, we should think of reasons as making options eligible, and making their choice intelligible, rather than as strictly speaking requiring actions. This avoided the need to distinguish between optional reasons and requiring reasons. There is only one kind of reasons for action. They require action if the reasons for it defeat those for any alternative, and they merely make the action intelligible *vis à vis* alternatives the reasons for which are not defeated by them.

This, however, fails to explain why sometimes we must take a certain action, so that if we do not we act wrongly, whereas at other times even though the reasons for the action defeat those for any alternative (e.g., I have better reason to see the new Tarantino film tonight than to do anything else we can do tonight) yet failing to take it is not wrong (if I fail to go to Tarantino my action may be unwise, lazy, weak-willed, etc., but not wrong). The discussion of respect in chapter 4 is meant to be a beginning of an explanation of when reasons are wrong-making, and when not. I suppose that deep down that is the part of the book which seems most important to me. It draws a distinction between two ways of relating to what is valuable, respecting it and engaging with it. We must respect what is valuable and it is wrong not to do so. We have reason to engage with what is valuable, and it is intelligible that we should do so. Sometimes it is foolish, rash, weak, defective in some other specific way, or even irrational to fail to engage with what is of greater value than available alternatives, or to engage with what is of lesser value. But it is not, generally speaking, wrong to do so.

How do these reflections relate to maximisation? I believe it is a mistake to think that the theses about the universality of values and about the value–reason nexus in and of themselves commit one to a maximising attitude to practical rationality, that is, to the view that one's overall rational commitment is to take those actions which of all the options open to one maximise expected value. The value–reason nexus commits one to no more than that one should always take the best action available. It is not committed to the view that there is anything to maximise. That is, it is not committed to the view that the best action is the one which is expected to produce most good, or which will realise most good or which would maximally promote the good. For it is not committed to the view that it as much as makes sense to talk of maximising good or value, or of promoting value or the good, or of realising most good.

Of course, such expressions have their use in certain contexts. It may make sense to talk of maximising economic value, or promoting or maximising educational opportunities, or of maximising people's chances of staying alive longer, and so

6

on. But if my choice is between attending a good performance of Janacek's *Jenufa*, or reading Gerry Cohen's new book, or joining a dance party, it does not seem to me to make sense to ask myself which of these will promote or produce most good or value, or which will maximise good. The three are all intrinsically valuable activities in their various ways (and they probably also have instrumental benefits and drawbacks which we can disregard here). It is possible that one of them is a better action, or a more valuable one, but that would not be because it maximises good or value.

Where a single person is concerned, it would seem that maximisation is at home when we consider certain kinds of valuable options, and not others. Probably it is most at home when the goods concerned are either instrumental goods (I can maximise my economic resources, etc.) or when they are conditions for achieving some goods (e.g. maximising my educational opportunities). They seem to be out of place when we deal with intrinsic goods affecting a single person. Maximising considerations are, however, often at home when we deal with several persons and compare benefits or harms to several of them. It is difficult to avoid the thought that numbers count and that, to take an easy case, if the choice is between conferring a particular benefit on one person or conferring the very same benefit on two we should confer it on two. I have nothing to say here about interpersonal maximisation.

I highlight the bearing of chapter 4 on the debate about reason and maximisation, for that aspect of it does not take centre stage in the way the chapter is structured and presented. It continues the sequence, starting with chapter 3 on the value of staying alive, of discussions of issues at the foundations of central areas of morality. My focus in both is on the central theme of the book, that is, the reconciliation of the universality of value with its social dependence, and with partiality. Life, respect for people, and personal well-being are paradigmatic examples of what people tend to regard as universal values. My argument is that staying alive is not of value to the person whose life it is, but rather a precondition of anything good or bad happening to him. The duty of respect for people, though a universal duty, arising out of the fact that people are of value in themselves, derives its concrete manifestations from social practices. In brief, the foundational moral values are universally valid in abstract form but they manifest themselves in ways which are socially dependent, and become accessible to us in ways which are socially dependent.

The role of partiality and its relation to universality are central to chapter 4. The doctrine of respect, with the difference it assumes between respecting what is valuable and engaging with it, is meant to explain the limits of partiality, that is, that partiality is permissible so long as it does not conflict with respect for what is valuable, respect being, as I mentioned above, within the domain of reasons whose violation is wrong. The discussion of respect explains the contours and limits of partiality in one's own cause.

I prepared for the Seeley lectures by presenting drafts of these lectures to my students at Columbia both in the Fall of 1998 (in a joint seminar with Jeremy Waldron) and in a much more complete and elaborate form during the Fall of 1999, and was helped in revising them for publication by presenting the texts of the lectures for comment and criticism in a seminar I ran jointly with Ulrike Heuer in Oxford in the spring of 2000. A much shorter version of chapter 1 was presented at Stanford as part of a Presidential symposium on Past Dependence in November 1999, and chapter 3 was given as a paper at an MIT philosophy colloquium. I benefited from all the discussions during those occasions, but would like to single out for special thanks the penetrating criticism of Charles Beitz, Ken Ehrenberg, David Enoch, David Friar, Malte Gethold, Scott Hershowitz, Jeff Seidman, Dale Smith, Jeremy Waldron, and especially Ulrike Heuer, whose detailed criticism of all the papers during our joint seminar and in private conversations helped me to improve many aspects of the original lectures, and saved me from many mistakes. I fear that none of them will think that I learnt all the lessons they tried to teach me. I know, however, that I learnt much from them as well as, as always, from conversations with and comments from Penelope Bulloch. Even though I did not have the opportunity to discuss this book with him I owe a debt of gratitude to Don Regan, with whom I have been debating the relations between personal well-being and other values whenever we met over a long period since sometime in the early 1980s, and most especially during a short joint seminar at Ann Arbor in 1994. Over the years, sometimes imperceptibly, my views have shifted towards his. His example of sustained struggle with some of these problems has been inspiring.

1

Attachment and uniqueness

> The crucial issue is not whether sentiments and attitudes
> are seen as important . . . , but whether – and to what
> extent – these sentiments and attitudes can be influenced
> and cultivated through reasoning.[1]

Having left the *morally* worst century of human history[2] we
may on occasion seek solace by reflecting on aspects of the recent past which can count as moral advances, as pointers to a
more decent future for our species. When my mind turns to
such thoughts perhaps one feature stands out. I will call it the
legitimation of difference. I have in mind a change in sensibility, a change in what people find obvious and what appears to
them to require justification and explanation. Such changes are
never universal. This one may not have gone very far yet. But
I think, and hope, that there has been such a shift in the moral
sensibility of many people in the West, a shift towards taking
difference – in culture and religion, in gender, sexual orienta-
tion or in race – for granted, acknowledging its unquestioned
legitimacy, and seeking justification only when hostility to

---

[1] A. Sen, 'East and West: The Reach of Reason' *New York Review of Books*,
vol. 47, No. 12, 20/7/2000.
[2] Cf. Jonathan Glover, *Humanity: A Moral History of the Twentieth Century*
(London: Jonathan Cape, 1999).

difference is manifested, or where advantage is given to one side of such divides.[3]

Is it evidence of that shift, or is it proof of the vitality of the Seeley lectures, that all previous lecturers devoted so much attention to diversity and disagreement and the proper response to them? For surely such shifts in sensibility breed, as well as being nourished by, shifts in theoretical reflection. The questions I wish to explore in these lectures have acquired greater importance and topicality because of their implications for the theoretical reflections accompanying the legitimation of difference. The views that many take on the matters I will discuss are motivated by their response to the legitimation of difference. However, I feel that we do best when we keep the inquiry within its proper theoretical boundaries and will, therefore, refrain for the most part from drawing any 'practical' implications from the reflections that follow.

Accepting the legitimacy of difference is theoretically problematic. The acceptance is more than a matter of acknowledging facts. It consists in endorsing certain evaluative attitudes to normative practices. Difference is multifaceted and so is the reaction to it. It is hard to generalise without distorting. But roughly it means endorsing affirming, approving attitudes to normative practices which often appear inconsistent, or even

---

[3] My optimism on that score is accompanied by growing anxiety at the increase in self-righteous intolerance which seems to be gaining ground in the USA and in Britain, manifesting itself in pride in zero-tolerance policies, and vindictive hostility towards anyone who fails to conform to the prevailing view of the day. Could it be that while we gain in moral sensibility on some fronts we lose on others?

positively hostile to each other. The diversity of religious beliefs is an obvious example. But so are the divergent lifestyles associated with many cultural and other differences. These apparent inconsistencies give rise to acute practical problems. And I will keep my promise not to discuss them here. They also give rise to theoretical puzzles. How can we consistently believe in the legitimacy of difference? Some think that it must lead to embracing subjectivist, or emotivist, or projectivist understandings of morality. Others are drawn to one or another form of ethical or value relativism as the reconciling view. This relativistic response often includes the rejection of any belief in the universality of values. For many the rejection of the universality of values is the very essence of relativism. My topic in the next chapter will be an exploration of the boundaries of coherent relativism.

In this chapter I wish to examine a different challenge to the thesis that values are universal. The challenge is that the universality thesis fails to explain our deepest attachments, the attachments of love and friendship, for example, or of the relations between parents and children, or people and their countries, attachments without which life does not have meaning. In resisting this challenge I will rely for assistance on *The Little Prince*.

1 Loss of innocence: destruction of meaning or liberation?

I want to start at a moment of crisis. Here is how it is described:

> All roads lead to the abodes of men. 'Good morning', he said. He was standing before a garden all a-bloom with

roses. 'Good morning', said the roses. The little prince looked at them. They all looked like his flower. 'Who are you?' he demanded, thunderstruck. 'We are roses', said the roses. And he was overcome with sadness . . . 'I thought [the little prince reflected] that I was rich, with a flower that was unique in all the world; and all I had was a common rose . . . That does not make me a very great prince.' And he lay down . . . and cried.[4]

It is a sweet story of a universal experience. We become aware of the world, if we are lucky, in the bosom of strong attachments. They are formative of our capacity to sustain attachments, personal and others, which are, for each of us, *unique* and understood to be so. Gradually the world opens in front of us, and the objects of our attachments lose their uniqueness. It is a moment of crisis. To survive and prosper we need to be able to reconcile deep identity-defining attachments, with the realisation that the objects of these attachments may not be all that unique. Neither Saint-Exupéry nor I have anything to say about the psychology of this adjustment. But, while sometimes using psychological idiom in a metaphorical way, I will strive to follow the Little Prince with some remarks about the nature of the resolution.

Am I not making too much of the so-called crisis which the Little Prince faces? Is it not a simple case of growing up? This is how a familiar story goes: both individually and as a species we mature by transcending the particular and moving towards the universal; as we, individually, and as a species, grow up our

---

[4] Antoine de Saint-Exupéry, *The Little Prince*, tr. by Katherine Woods (London: Mammoth, 1931), pp. 60–2.

horizons broaden, we come to understand more aspects of the world, and to understand better our situation in the world. Just like the Little Prince we transcend the confines of our birth, and the attachments of our infancy and childhood. We realise that there are other people like our parents, others like ourselves.

We come to recognise and to submit to the inescapable power of reason. Its judgement is harsh. It is a hard but necessary lesson to learn that we are not entitled to anything just because we are we, and our loved ones are not special just because they are ours. But reason also liberates us from the narrow confines of our birth. It opens up the world, enabling us to move within it, free citizens of the universe, whose rights of passage are recognised by all those likewise possessed of reason.

This is not the way the Little Prince resolves his crisis, but it is a familiar enough story, and a very powerful one. Can it be denied that just as individuals become moral agents worthy of respect only when they grow to acknowledge that they are each just one among many, all entitled to consideration, so we, as a species, advanced morally by overcoming arbitrary boundaries and allegiances, by recognising that people generally, that animals generally, deserve consideration and their interests should not be ignored? Has not the use of political power improved by being governed by rational universal principles, by having transcended tribal allegiances and various other kinds of personal and group favouritism?

I think that the Little Prince will not be able to deny that there is much truth in all that, but these facts will not help him overcome his crisis. He believes in the importance of uniqueness. He believes that uniqueness is of the nature of love, which is for him the paradigm of all special attachments to people and to objects. He believes that both meaning and understanding, misery and happiness, arise out of one's special, particular, non-universal, attachments. In the words he later learns from the Fox: 'one only understands the things that one tames' – taming being the Fox's way of conceptualising special particularised attachments to people or other objects. The Fox has a whole theory of attachments. His applies primarily to loving personal relations, but can be extended *mutatis mutandis* to relations to objects, causes, institutions, countries, cultures, works of art, one's profession or anything else:

> 'My life is monotonous', he said, 'I hunt chickens; men hunt me. All the chickens are just alike, and all men are just alike . . . I am a little bored. But if you tame me it will be as if the sun came to shine on my life. I shall know the sound of a step that will be different from all the others . . . Yours will call me, like music . . . And then look: you see the grain fields . . . You have hair . . . the colour of gold. Think now how wonderful that will be when you have tamed me. The grain, which is also golden, will bring me back the thought of you and I shall love to listen to the wind in the wheat.' (pp. 64–5)

What a naïve optimist, you may say. Doesn't he know that love can flounder and is the source of misery as well as of happiness? But the Fox is no wide-eyed dreamer. His romanticism embraces all facets of life. There is value in sadness and disappointment. They have value because they too can be meaningful elements in one's life. But even when failure and sadness are purely negative elements in a life, their existence is a by-product of the possibility of positive meaning: there is no possibility of success without a possibility of failure, no possibility of positive personal meaning without the possibility of negative value.

Meaning is invested in the world by our attachments to it: meaning rests primarily in the objects of our attachments, and by association in other things. There may be an exaggeration here, but surely there is truth too. The view the Fox's observations suggest is one according to which attachments to objects, all attachments, confer value on their objects, and on others associated with them, whatever these objects may be. There are three exaggerations here. First, not all attachments can confer value on their objects, only valuable attachments do so. Second, the Fox exaggerates, because not all value, and that is part of what we have in mind in 'meaning', can derive from attachments. Third, the Fox intimates a general connection between attachments and uniqueness whereas only some attachments involve uniqueness. This last point may be my exaggeration, rather than the Fox's. He is not explicit on how far one can generalise his account of 'taming'. I will consider this point in section 3 below. The first two exaggerations are closely interconnected. Because not all value derives from attachment, some attachments can lack value, that is they can be worthless to the person whose attachments they are. To be of value to the people whose attachments they are attachments must be valuable in themselves.[5] Let me explain.

---

[5] In the text of the chapter I use 'attachments' to refer both to particular attachments of particular individuals, and to kinds or types of attachments, relying on context to clarify the meaning. The claim made in the text above is that the value of attachments of a certain kind does not depend exclusively on the fact that those whose attachments they are embrace them willingly or with approval. This is consistent with the fact

We cannot form attachments, and we cannot sustain those we have, except where *we think* that doing so is worthwhile, that is, in the belief that there is value in having the attachments or in forming them. In part this is merely a clarification of the sense in which the term is used here: it refers only to ties of which we are conscious, and it excludes those we find ourselves burdened with against our will, those we would rather be without but from which we cannot, at least not without much effort, shake ourselves free. Our attachments are endorsed by us, and that means that they are seen as valuable.[6] We may, of course, be wrong, and this or that attachment may be devoid of value.

that the value of attachments of that kind depends in part, at least normally, on the attitude of people who are so attached. Their impersonal value, referred to in the text, is their value to one were they to be one's attachments, which is independent of the fact that they were embraced by one as one's attachments.

The 'personal value' of an attachment is a value of a concrete attachment to the person who has it. That its value depends on the person's attitude to the object or objective of the attachment is part, but only a part, of the case for my claim that personal attachments give meaning to people's lives. People derive a sense of purpose and of value in their life from their engagements with pursuits and relationships that they regard, implicitly or explicitly, as worthwhile, that is, from their attachments.

[6] This claim should be read as being compatible with some irrational, and even pathological, and self-destructive attachments. Sometimes people form or maintain attachments against their better judgement, and keep them alive even when they cause them much suffering. But much of the time this is done because of the overpowering attraction of some good aspect of the relationship, say, sexual attraction, or the comfort of familiarity and security (which can persist even in the presence of physical or mental abuse), etc. Though obviously some pathologies do not conform to this pattern, and some attachments are maintained purely out of fear.

17

But much of the time our mistakes are contingent. We have no reason to think that these beliefs *must* be wrong, that it is never good to have attachments, or that we can never know when it is.

It is possible for people to form an attachment thinking that it will be valuable just because they formed it, or that they formed it in certain circumstances, quite independent of the nature and value of its object. Perhaps some attachments are valuable for such reasons. But these are highly unusual cases. For the most part we form and maintain attachments believing in the suitability of their objects. We do not fall in love because we have reason to fall in love with this person and with no other, but we believe that the people we love are suitable objects of our love. Otherwise the love is demeaning to us, is an obsession we cannot rid ourselves of, a weakness we fail to struggle against, or an expression of some other pathology. This also shows that we generally believe that the value of our attachments depends on the suitability of their objects, and that attachments to unsuitable objects can be valueless.[7] Here

---

[7] That is, without any value at all (rather than that on balance their down side is greater than their value). I have seen this suggestion doubted on the ground that it is inconsistent with the spontaneity and the autonomy of our emotions. It is as if one said that one's love is worthwhile only if the person one loves is the most suitable person one can love, or as if one has to deserve to be loved. But that is not the meaning of my claim. It does not imply anything about what makes one a suitable object of an attachment. It may be that one is capable of reciprocating, and nothing more, that one would not abuse it, or any other test. It all depends on the nature of the attachment and of its object. But clearly one can be a suitable object of love, even if the love is not successful, or even if there are others such that had one loved them instead one would have fared better, etc.

again there is nothing awry with our beliefs. They express the structure of our concepts, and establish the first exaggeration in the Fox's implied position. In general, an attachment must have a worthy object to be valuable.

But while the Fox is wrong about value and meaning in general, he is right if *personal meaning* is what he has in mind, that is, the meaning which is personal to each of us, and which can make our life worth living. Personal meaning does indeed depend on attachments: we live for our relations with people we love, for the goals we pursue, be they professional, political, social, or other, and for those aspects of the world which have come to have special meaning for us, those we have 'tamed'. If you doubt that, try and revive the spirits of a depressed or suicidal person by pointing out how much of value there is in the world: mention the beauty of nature, treasures of supreme art filling the museums, the wealth of sublime music, the great number of lovers, etc. One is more likely to drive such a person further into gloom. Their problem is not the absence of value in the world but the absence of meaning in their life. Personal meaning, as the Fox says, derives from attachments.

How then does the personal meaning of attachments and their objects relate to their (impersonal) value? Simply: our attachments appropriate (impersonal) value, and make it meaningful for us. They go well beyond the recognition of the value of their objects, and of the attachments themselves. They endow it with a role in our lives, make it relevant to the success or failure of our life. I may recognise the merits of my city, and the value of engaging in civic activities, but only my actual embracing that good by caring about and becoming actively involved in the civic life of my city makes the life of my city, and my engagement with it, important for the success of my own life. The personal meaning of objects, causes, and pursuits depends on their impersonal value, and is conditional on it. But things of value have to be appropriated by us to endow our lives with meaning, meaning which is a precondition for life being either a success or a failure. Attachments are the name I give here to these appropriations; they are the results of the taming the Fox explains to his new friend.

2 Taming: desire or common history

Corrupted by utilitarians and by some economists we may think that our desires invest what we desire with personal meaning. The Little Prince, having learnt his lesson, knows better. Addressing the roses in the rose garden he says:

> You are not at all like my rose. As yet you are nothing. No one has tamed you, and you have tamed no one ... You are beautiful, but you are empty ... One could not die for you ... [My rose] is more important than all the hundreds of you ... because it is she that I have watered; because it is she that I have sheltered ... because it is for her that I have killed the caterpillars ... because it is she that I have listened to, when she grumbled, or boasted, or even sometimes when she said nothing. Because she is *my* rose. (p. 68)

Meaning comes through a common history, and through work. They make the object of one's attachment unique. You will not be surprised that meaning comes with responsibility and through responsibility. By assuming duties we create attachments. Duties and special responsibilities, not rights, are the key to a meaningful life, and are inseparable from it. In denying our duties we deny the meaning of our life.

Of course not all duties are like that. Not all of them arise out of our attachments, out of our partiality for some things. Some duties are independent of such attachments. Some, as we will see when we get to discuss respect for people in chapter 4, are based on the impersonal value of things, and are a precondition for our capacity to form attachments. But personal meaning depends on attachments which are constituted in part by the duties we incur in the course of our life, as a result of the way our life unfolds.

Why duties rather than rights? Because duties involve responsibilities and, therefore, engage our lives in a way which rights do not.[8] We are passive regarding our rights, we are recipients so far as they are concerned. We may benefit from them even while we are totally unaware of them. We may of course conform with our duties without being aware of them either. But this normally only means that we do not refer to them in deliberation. I do not consider my duty to care for my child when I care for my child. I do not consider the duty not to murder before I say hello to a person without murdering him. It does not follow that the duty to care for my child or that the prohibition on murder does not shape my actions. Duties are reasons for action. They can shape our view of our options even when we do not deliberate, or do not refer to them in our deliberations. For most of us, our duty not to murder

---

[8] Cf. my 'Liberating Duties' in J. Raz, *Ethics in the Public Domain* (Oxford: Oxford University Press, 1995).

makes the thought of murder inconceivable. Our duties rule out many options – exclude them from our mental horizon. This is a way of guiding our life, perhaps the deepest and most profound way.

Rights too can have such an aspect. Some rights determine status: establish that one is a citizen, or just a member of a society, and so on. Consciousness of them may be important to our sense of who we are. Yet, unless the status brings with it duties, and therefore responsibilities, rights are less intimately engaged with our life. Our duties define our identities more profoundly than do our rights. They are among the primary constituents of our attachments, among the fundamental contributors to meaning in our life.

3 What kind of uniqueness, when, and why?

The Little Prince's spirits revive. His rose is not perceptually unique, but unique she is, made unique by the history of their love.

At this point I should confess some unease with the way the Little Prince solves his crisis. He has what is to me, personally, an unappetising taste for an ethereal, disembodied, aesthetic. Many value people and objects for being perceptually unique, that is, reliably identifiable by sight (normally) or by sound or another sense. The Little Prince resolves his crisis by rejecting the importance of unique perceptual identifiability, and, one suspects, downgrading the importance of all perceptual and sensual properties. From now on it matters not to him that his rose is visually indistinguishable from others.

Their shared history makes it unique and that is good enough. All I can say is, this may be fine for him, but need not be fine for everyone.

He loved his rose for her looks, and having discovered that she is not unique in her looks he now realises that he was mistaken and that his love was based on their common history. This kind of transmutation of love, its survival even as its self-understanding changes, is common, and, far from being objectionable, may be necessary in the conditions of our lives. Lasting relationships are, typically, not those which remain unchanged for many years, but rather those which do change, where the relationship acquires new meanings with time, to replace the value which faded away, as well as those which, though founded on misperceptions and plain mistakes about oneself or the other, retain their vitality once the mistakes come to light, through a better understanding of what they really mean to oneself or the other. My personal reservations with the Little Prince's new understanding of his love have to do with the suggestion that loving the rose for her looks is shallow, or even that it is a self-defeating foundation for love, liable to lead to its death upon the discovery that others are just as beautiful.

The life of many people is enriched by their loving attachments to people or other objects based on their looks, or on other of their perceived characteristics. We know that many deep friendships and many loving relations are cemented by attraction to the looks, smell, or feel to the touch of the other. In some circles this is sniffed at. But it should not be. People's looks, as well as all aspects of their sensuality, are among their most important characteristics, to be valued by them, and by others.[9]

But is not the Little Prince right that people's perceptual characteristics are not unique to them, and thus cannot form the foundation for an attachment, since attachments presuppose uniqueness? Perceptual and sensual qualities can be *de facto* unique, or unique for all practical purposes, that is, extremely unlikely to be replicated in the experience of the people concerned.[10] Such *de facto* uniqueness is often of crucial importance to people, and for good reasons.[11] It is true, however, that logical uniqueness may be important as well, and a common history is the only practical way to ensure it.

[9] The anti-sensual tendency in some parts of contemporary culture combines with the belief that people's looks, and their other sensual properties, are less worthwhile, and their possession is no merit in their possessors because they are an accident of nature, not a result of the will or decision of their possessors (though oddly many sniff even more at those who spend much effort to improve their looks). The fallacy that merit or desert arises only out of choice or effort of will is one of the great vices of much intellectual work in ethics and political philosophy today. But that is a story for another occasion.

[10] Where our capacity to discern differences under so-called normal conditions determines the degree of similarity which will defeat a claim to uniqueness.

[11] Typically the reasons combine the fact that most people rely on perceived properties for recognition with the fact that in the culture we inhabit recognition has to be fairly instantaneous or it will evoke loss of confidence in the attachment on both sides (that these points are subject to exceptions regarding people with perceptual or recognitional disabilities does not show that they do not apply to those who do not have those disabilities). This is combined with the special value that perceived properties may have in the relationship.

The most abstract and basic reason for the importance of (logical) uniqueness is that attachments, attachments of the kind we are considering,[12] are to a particular individual, who is irreplaceable. Of course, this does not mean that one cannot have more than one attachment, only that they are different, and not fungible. As when, having lost a child, one has another, or as one falls in love again after an earlier relationship with a lover went sour, one attachment may come to fill a gap left by the demise of another, but it will not be quite the same, even if it is no less good, or even if it is better overall, than the other.

Irreplaceability is, of course, aspect dependent. Every thing is irreplaceable in some respects, and replaceable in others. In many contexts assertions of irreplaceability refer to the value of the allegedly irreplaceable object. But they do not mean that the object is irreplaceable because its value is greater than that of any possible replacement (most commonly this will be asserted by saying that the object is 'incomparable'). They may mean that *in some aspect* it is better than any possible replacement. But often they mean something rather different, namely that there is (or was) something about the object which lends

---

[12] Earlier I suggested that the Fox's account of taming, of appropriating universal value and creating personal meaning, can be generalised well beyond loving relationships to all attachments. I believe this to be so, but uniqueness does not play a role in all of them. It is typically important when the attachment is to an object or a person. In such cases the value of the attachment often presupposes the uniqueness of its object, i.e., the value of the attachment is predicated on a unique relationship of the subject to that particular object. The same is not typical of attachments to causes, or types of activities. Sometimes their unique role or place in the life of the subject is part of their value. But often it is not.

it value of a special kind, such that while some feasible replacements may be as good or even better, they will not be quite the same – not quite the same in what makes them good or valuable, and in the precise way they are or were good or valuable. It is this sense which is relevant to the understanding of why (logical) uniqueness is sometimes important in attachments.

Think of parents' attachment to their child. Assume that it is reasonably successful, and is of a fairly common kind. The parents regard the child as irreplaceable. They need not deny that if the child died they would have another, and that for all they know their relation with the new child would be as successful and rewarding. Acknowledging this they still regard the child as irreplaceable. Nor is this feeling simply an expression of their desire to be spared the pain and anguish of experiencing the death of their child and their anxiety before their new one is born and their relationship with him or her proves successful. Suppose all this happens, and now, happy with their new child, they look back. They still think of their relationship with the first child as unique and think that the child was irreplaceable. There was something special in their relationship with their dead child which makes it different, and different in the way it was good, from their relationship with their new child.

All this is compatible with the relationship with the dead child having been unique only *de facto*. It was made of many factors, all of them in principle reproducible, but in fact extremely unlikely to be repeated. It is possible that such *de facto* uniqueness is all that the parents value. But not atypically this is not the case. We cannot test this with realistic scenarios, but we will not be surprised that faced with an imaginary scenario of replacing their child with another such that all the valuable aspects of the child and their relations with him are replicated they will reject the option, on the ground that their attachment to their current child is unique and irreplaceable. If the replacement takes place anyway they will regret the loss of their first child, in spite of the arrival of an equally good replacement.[13] Given the artificiality of this scenario we may not wish to place much weight on it. Even if such reactions are not uncommon they may be confused, or otherwise unwarranted.

Indeed, it is not my claim that all relationships with people, or that all attachments to objects, must be unique to be valuable. But that they often are can be seen in the fact that features which make them (logically) unique in the life of the people whose attachments they are, are part of their value. The first child was the parents' first, and that makes the attachment special, gives it a flavour no other can have for them. Not that relations with a first child are always good. They can be bad, and the child being the first one may make things worse. But when the relationship with the child is good, that it was their first child may be part of what makes the relationship special for the parents (and for the child) and gives it special flavour, a special value which for them is unrepeatable, a value which cannot be exhaustively described in terms of properties which are in principle repeatable in their life.

The object of an attachment is unique if one of its properties, essential to the value it in fact has, and which is

---

[13] I am not imagining two qualitatively identical children. This will raise other questions, not relevant here. In the example under discussion the replacement child is simply identical in the in-principle-repeatable (in the life of the parents) good-making characteristics.

responsible for at least part of the value of the attachment to it, is such that it can only be instantiated once.[14] This is the conceptual explanation why the object is unique.[15] What we are more interested in is a psychological explanation of whether, and if so why, attachments of this kind are so central to the meaning of our life, as I suspect they are. Unfortunately, I do not have anything illuminating to say about that.

[14] Notice that it is the object we are attached to, not the features which make the attachment valuable. But that fact does not solve the problem of uniqueness. Of course, the object has a particular, not a general property. But, as we see it, we are attached to it for some reason or other. The attachment is not a fact we discover about ourselves, it is an attitude we endorse. (Though, as mentioned above, we can be obsessively or addictively attached against our will, or without understanding what it is that keeps us attached to an object.) The problem of uniqueness arises out of the fact that we have reasons for the attachments we are talking about, and that reasons are universal (see more in chapter 2 below).

   That does not mean that the uniqueness of the object is what is valuable or valued about it. Were this so then the object, and the attachment to it, would have been replaceable, since there are other objects which are unique. If what was of value was having an attachment to a unique object then others would have done just as well. Rather the uniqueness of the valuable properties of the attachment makes it irreplaceable whether or not one values its uniqueness.

   The way of understanding the unique value of certain personal attachments I offer here, i.e., via the value of historical properties, can capture the sense in which what is uniquely valuable is the object – it is the object under that historical description: my first child, i.e., my child qua a first child, etc.

[15] It also explains why the requirement of uniqueness is not empty. To be sure, everything is unique in some ways, but the ways which count are those which make for the value of the attachment and not everything is unique in such ways.

Cases where the perceptual features of a person or object are at the core of the attachment represent a special case. Two elements mark them. First, it is normally[16] important to people to be able perceptually to identify those they are attached to. Second, perceptual properties are not unique. Different people may look the same, etc. The combination of the two means that some attachments persist and thrive because as a matter of fact the object of the attachment is unique in the experience of the person who is attached to it. Such attachments will be shattered or transformed if a perceptually indistinguishable object appears. Discovering that the object of one's affection has a perceptually indistinguishable identical twin, can put a great strain on a relationship. The discovery that one's favourite painting is visually indistinguishable from a replica can also have an unsettling effect.

In such cases *de facto* perceptual uniqueness may also be a condition for the existence and success of the attachment. But this requirement of *de facto* perceptual uniqueness, that is, of being able perceptually to identify the object of one's attachment among objects within one's experience, is distinct from the basic requirement of logical uniqueness mentioned before, and is due to the specific nature of these attachments. It is consistent with the fact that strict and not merely *de facto* uniqueness defines this type of attachment, provided that the object of the attachment possesses additional valuable properties which are unique and which contribute to the value of the attachment.

[16] There are exceptions to this generalisation: a blind person may be in love with another because of their good looks, even if he or she cannot see them for themselves, just as they can be attached to a painting because of its appearance, though they cannot see it.

Here the Fox's explanation comes to the rescue. Valuing objects for their (*de facto*) unique looks does not conflict with the Fox's theory of attachments. Attachments to people or other objects are forged by common history, by assumption of responsibility, and the rest. But some *also* involve valuing the *de facto* unique looks of their objects.

Is this a genuine solution to the crisis? Or does the central importance of personal attachments only make the crisis worse? Personal attachments to objects, we learn, characteristically derive their value in part from the uniqueness of the object or the attachment to the person whose attachment it is. The Little Prince is now convinced that even though the roses in the garden are in their intrinsic qualitative properties – and I hope he will forgive me this mouthful – indistinguishable from *his* rose, nevertheless his rose is unique, unique to him. Its uniqueness is not in its intrinsic and qualitative properties. It is past dependent. It is in its, and his, past actions and decisions.

Personal attachments emerge through our biographies, and where their value depends on unique biographical features, they are unique to each one of us. Is this the solution to the puzzle? Before we probe further let us turn our attention from the personal to the public, for, of course, the problem of the standing of uniqueness faces us in public life as much as in private.

4 A public diversion

There are two sides to the public story, a reassuring side, and a worrying part. The reassurance is that people's past actions can be and often are given their due in public action: war veterans, say, or people with partners, can be and often are rightly treated in special ways because of their past actions. The Little Prince's attachment to *his* rose can be given public recognition, for the law, or the public domain more broadly, can acknowledge that every attachment, or every attachment meeting some conditions, shall be recognised as a source of status, rights, or responsibilities.

This will put to rest one misconceived fear, namely that personal attachments, being unique, are arbitrary. It shows that recognition of the value of unique attachments meets the condition of universalisability, and that it is intelligible: we can understand it because we can subsume it under general concepts, concepts which explain the good in it, the value of such attachments. This is no surprise: in our informal way that is what the Fox and I have been doing by relating attachments to the meaning life has for people.

Furthermore – a point of no little importance – the public recognition of *personal* attachments can be impartial: The attachments are each unique to each individual, but others, like them in value and significance, can and often do exist in the life of other people. The public domain can accord recognition to all such attachments impartially.

But, beginning to worry, we may wonder: is this enough? Impartiality is preserved in the public domain so long as the state – which I shall mention as the agent dominating the public domain, though clearly other agents are involved as well – acts as an impartial adjudicator, self-effacing, and lacking a character of its own. But that is not the way states normally act. They regard themselves as custodians of a national heritage. They protect historical sites, aspects of the natural environment, cultural treasures, languages, and the works created in them, and more. Let us take an example, from far off, so that our personal attachments will not get too much in the way.

I will talk about education, though similar considerations would apply to any cultural activity supported, directly or indirectly, by our public agents. Pär Lagerkvist does, I imagine, loom large in the curriculum in Sweden. A similar prominence, let me assume, is given to the writings of Frans Eemil Sillanpää in Finland. Suppose that a protest is raised, demanding the demotion of Sillanpää and giving more time to Lagerkvist, on the ground that he is the greater writer. When disputes like this arise they often lead to debates about who is the greater novelist, how objective are such judgements, and what are the criteria of literary value. These are important and stimulating questions, but they need not be involved. One can acknowledge that Lagerkvist is the greater writer, and yet resist the suggestion that Sillanpää should take second place to him on the ground – for these purposes I am a Finn – that Sillanpää is ours, whereas Lagerkvist is not. To reject this claim is to hold that there is a first league of world authors: Shakespeare, Goethe, Balzac, Tolstoy, Proust, and whoever, who should furnish the material for the curriculum everywhere, never mind whether this is Germany or Albania, and so on. This attitude is the recipe for the destruction of cultures and traditions, for the greatest standardisation of civilisation, a standardisation so far achieved only in the big corporate hotel chains: the Hiltons, the Holiday Inns, and their like.

5 Attachments and identity

But what is wrong with the dream of a universal culture of high achievement? Why should Sillanpää be taught in Finland just because he was a Finn? To answer that is to understand what it is to be a Finn, or a Swede, or anything else.[17] A point which brings us back to the so far neglected connection between attachment and identity. So let me go back from the public to the personal.

We can take certain things as understood. For example, that when talking of 'identity' I do not mean the term in the sense in which it fixes the limits to the continuity of an object, or an object of a kind: is this pile of timber which made up Theseus' boat Theseus' boat still? We mean the identity revealed in answers to the question who am I? I am a man, an academic, a father, etc. These make me who I am. It is the identity that identity politics is about which is, in part, determined by our past actions and decisions. It is the identity which leads one to say: 'Here I stand, I can do no other', in the knowledge that one could if one wanted to, and yet one is speaking the truth. It is a truth which may be thrust upon one, rather than be made by one. Being Jewish is not a matter of choice for me, nor being of a dark complexion, nor being a man. But some aspects of one's identity are a product of one's life, freely chosen or otherwise, such as being an immigrant, or an academic.

---

[17] Note that the argument applies only to aspects of a culture which are, and only inasmuch as they are, of intrinsic value. Those which are instrumentally valuable may not be regarded as a cultural or national possession. Therefore the argument does not imply that different science should be studied in different countries.

There are distinctions here which we can take as read. Perhaps being a lover of this rose is not part of the identity of the Little Prince, but being a lover certainly is.[18] In general only the more abstract of one's attachments are identity-forming: one's craving to have a regular abode, or to be a nomad through life, rather than one's love of one's current abode, or current journeys. Though this is only a matter of degree. There is no sharp boundary between identity-forming and other attachments.

All aspects of one's identity become a positive force in one's life only if embraced and accepted as such.[19] They are the sources of meaning in one's life, and sources of responsibilities: my special responsibilities are those of a citizen, a parent, a lover, an academic. They are normative because they engage our integrity. We must be true to who we are, true to it even as we try to change. Thus, identity-forming attachments are the organising principles of our life, the real as well as the imaginative. They give it shape as well as meaning. In all that, they are among the determinants of our individuality. And they are partly, to repeat, past dependent. I could have been a lawyer, remained in my original country, and so on. Probably I would have been none the worse for it, but I would have been different. My life would have had a different meaning, and I would have been answerable to different responsibilities. To deny our past is to be false to ourselves. This is justification enough for our dependence on our past.

---

[18] And being of this or that nationality, ethnicity, etc., usually are.

[19] Though in a different way, aspects of one's identity which one wishes to change play a different, but no less important, role in one's life.

6 Group identity

Back to the group, national groups, or other groups. They too have an identity which is determined through their actions and traditions; an identity defined by their culture, by their collective memory, and by their common responsibilities, and arising out of them. Collective identities, like individual characters, tend to be a mix of the good, the bad, and the indifferent. Our interest, however, is not in group identities in themselves, but in their role in individual life, and especially in the fact that they contribute to individual identity. This is no group-fetishism, no valuing of mystic collective entities at the expense of concern for humans. It is recognition of the dependence of personal identity and personal meaning on people's membership of, and identification with, a wide range of groups, national, religious, professional, and more.[20]

So we should be able to take a whole range of decisions in educational and cultural matters, with their considerable economic and other implications, for reasons of this kind: to sustain and develop 'our' culture and traditions. 'What is the problem?' I hope many of you are saying. For surely we do take such decisions for such reasons every day of the week and, as I have just argued, in doing so we serve the interest of people who are attached to the causes our decisions serve. These

[20] Identification should not be confused with approval. Just like membership, so too identification may be a condition opening the way to a most scathing criticism of the group. No one cares more about a group than its members and those identifying with it. That in itself is commonly recognised as qualifying them to be critical in ways to which outsiders are not thought to be entitled.

decisions are like any others: grounded in the need to serve the interest of people. They are comparable with providing a free health service to meet health needs people have. But this view is too simple. It ignores both some of the consequences and some of the reasons for action in support of attachments. Such actions do indeed serve the interests of people who have the attachments, but equally they tend to perpetuate them, to foster circumstances likely to lead to similar attachments by the young, and others. Moreover, the reasons people support causes they are attached to are not entirely instrumental. They believe in the value of those causes, and support them because of those beliefs, as something which is intrinsically right or good. Up to a point they must do so, for their attachment to those causes includes a need to express itself, often in the public domain, through action which fosters those causes.

Action supporting various attachments in the public domain can of course be moderated in recognition of the rights and interests of others. But people's primary reasons for supporting causes are not impartial. We pursue those attachments because they are our attachments, attachments in whose value we believe. The state or other groups, as agents separate from their members, act on behalf of their members, and for reasons which are valid reasons for their members. So they act to promote what their members, or if you like, they themselves are attached to, because of their attachments, and because of their belief in their value.

This is a thought that many find natural and others are uncomfortable with. It upholds a tradition, the latter say, just because it is there. It is conservative, and it cannot be rationally defended. In the public domain we are facing the analogue of the personal crisis confronting the Little Prince on his arrival at the rose garden.

7 An Israeli example to reduce discomfort

Before confronting the point we can reduce its discomfort. There are limits to the role of such considerations, to the legitimate role they can play in public decisions. One example will have to do here.[21] An Israeli Basic law declares that the State of Israel is a Jewish state. Israeli courts struggled with the implications of the law for their practice. The president of the Supreme Court, Mr Justice Barak, said that a Jewish state means a state which embraces the values which Judaism gave the world, namely (and I quote) 'the love of mankind, the sanctity of life, social justice, equity, protecting human dignity, the rule of law over the legislature, etc.' I think that he gave the statute the only acceptable interpretation. Notice that in the same sense France too can be a Jewish state. It too can embrace the values which Judaism gave to the world, namely the love of mankind, the sanctity of life, social justice, equity, protecting human dignity, the rule of law over the legislature, etc. Indeed, it may well be said that in that sense no state can be a morally good state unless it is a Jewish state. Does that show that Barak adopted the wrong interpretation? Did he not empty that article in the law of all meaning? No and yes. He

---

[21] I am borrowing here from my discussion of the same example in my contribution to M. Walzer, M. Loberbaum, and N. J. Zohar (eds.), *The Jewish Political Tradition*, vol. I, pp. 509–14 (New Haven: Yale University Press, 2000).

did empty the law of meaning, but it was the right thing to do. It would be wrong to suppose that on top of following justice, equity, dignity, and other universal values, Israeli law should follow some additional *specifically Jewish values*, which may conflict with justice or the other values, and compromise them. Of course, to the extent that the universal values Barak mentions, and others, do not dictate a uniquely correct way of organising social institutions, and human relations – and they always fail and leave large discretionary areas – Israel should follow its own traditions. But that is not the same as relying on such traditions at the expense of ethical values. Nor is it the same as preferring the traditions of one group in its population over those of other groups.

8 Concluding

Some people will still doubt the rational defensibility of relying on traditions in the public sphere, and on personal attachments in the private. Why do they feel discomfort? I have tried to give reassurance by pointing out that there is no threat here to the requirement of universalisability of value judgements. In the sense in which it is a valid requirement it is a precondition of intelligibility and rationality. It reflects the thought that whatever is of value can be explained to be so without the use of singular references. The good in attachments and traditions can be thus explained. Therefore, no such worries about the rationality of attachments afflict the Little Prince. Concrete attachments are good for those whose attachments they are; their value is within the sphere of personal meaning. The uniqueness of an object or pursuit established

38

by an attachment is uniqueness to one person, not uniqueness impersonally judged.

What, then, is the problem? Some people may be troubled by considerations reminiscent of Bernard Williams' 'one thought too many' argument.[22] The house is on fire, your lover is in one room, someone else is in another. You rush in and save your lover. To be right must your reason have been: doing so will not only save a life, but will also save a valuable relationship, a valuable attachment (and I do not know whether the same will be true if I save the other person first)? Surely not. To have thought so is to have one thought too many, says Williams, and it diminishes the purity of your attachment to your lover. And he is right about the thinking, about the hesitation, and the need to run through the argument in one's head. But is he right about the knowledge? Is it not the case that sometimes the demands of others prevail over the call of one's attachments, and that a rational agent has implicit knowledge of when this is so and when not, knowledge he relies on without deliberation, knowledge which guides his totally instinctive action? The Williams problem should not trouble us. Is there anything which should?

Personal meaning emerges through our personal and collective history in ways which defy two extremes. They defy the belief in immutable universal values, and they defy the dream of unfettered self-creation. Personal meaning emerges through the building of attachments to objects suitable to such relationships: love demeans the lover if bestowed on an unworthy object, admiration is ridiculous if directed to the

[22] See B. Williams in J. J. C. Smart and B. Williams, *Utilitariansim: For and Against* (London: Cambridge University Press, 1973).

commonplace, respect is perverted when those respected do not merit it. *Ally McBeal*'s John does not merely appear ridiculous. He is ridiculous when he bestows his love on a frog. But while attachments must find worthy objects to be valuable, they also enhance the value of their objects, make them special and (in cases of attachments to persons and objects) unique to those whose history binds them thus.

I feel that it is the need to keep this balance between preexisting value and self-created value which is one important source of unease with the thought that value, in the way it figures in personal meaning, is historically moulded. We tend to veer to the extreme of total immutability and independence of value, or to the extreme of self-creation of value, whereas the truth is that value is neither, and both.

2

Universality and difference

In the last chapter I examined one source of doubt about the universality of value. To put it crudely, among what matters to us most, many believe, are attachments which are unique because of the uniqueness of their objects. The value of those attachments is also unique. They have the value they have because they have the objects they have. Since their objects are unique so is their value. But the universality of value is incompatible with the thought that value is unique. Or so the challenge goes.

I acknowledged the importance of uniqueness in our lives, especially in our relations to people dear to us, and to some other objects. But I dismissed the thought that it is incompatible with any sensible view about the universality of values. I relied on the distinction between the value of things, and their value to us, which I also called their 'personal meaning'. Personal meanings can depend on the uniqueness to us of the object of our attachments. But that is consistent with the fact that the value of these attachments, as distinct from their value to us, is universal. Their value to us lies in properties of the attachments, including properties of their objects and their relations to us, which make them unique in our life, sometimes unique *de facto*, and sometimes necessarily unique. This is not to say that what is important or meaningful for us is to have a unique relationship or object.[1] Rather that the value of the

---

[1] Though sometimes this too may be the case.

41

object or the attachment to us lies in a complex property or set of properties which it possesses, which includes some which make it unique, and where this fact plays a part in making it meaningful and valuable to us. This can be so because it is generally, and, if you like, impersonally valuable that people should have relationships and attachments to objects which possess these properties. This reconciliation explains how it is that the *value* of our attachments explains their value *to us*. Their *value* makes our attachments intelligible to us, and to everyone else.

The main challenge to the universality of value comes from another direction. I suggested that it is a theoretical by-product of the legitimation of difference. It is due to the continuously nagging doubts posed by the fact of value disagreement, and of the diversity of the values that people practise.

I will start by defining a universalist thesis, and presenting a simple argument for it. I will then examine the degree to which this thesis fails to conform to some common views about the implications of value universalism, and the degree of pluralism it can accommodate.

To anticipate: my claim will be that values are universal, given a thin understanding of universality, and that is a concomitant of the intelligibility of values, that is, of the possibility of explaining and coming to understand what is good about any good-making property. To that extent the universality of values is an essential feature of all values, part of what it is to be a good-making property. However, there is abroad a much thicker understanding of universality which is invoked in talk about the universality of human rights, for example, and which is applied to values, or at any rate to moral values generally. So understood the precept of the universality of value is ill-defined. It is difficult, and probably impossible, to provide an abstract characterisation of it as a general feature of values, or of moral values. Rather, it is invoked as part of an argument against the existence of some moral values, or the validity of some alleged moral principles, which are thought of as not universal. Whether or not the invocation of the universality of moral values is successful and cogent when thus understood contextually, and in relation to a variety of specific moral arguments, does not matter to our purpose. What matters is that it should not be confused with any essential property of values or of moral values, and that it therefore cannot be used as part of a general argument against value pluralism.

1 The thesis

Value

A prefatory word about value. My use of the term is uninhibitedly inflationary. Any property which (necessarily) makes anything which possesses it good (or bad) at least to a degree is an evaluative property, standing for some value.[2] Somewhat more informatively, though less precisely, we could also say that every property whose presence in an item (action, person, institution, or anything else) can in itself make an action, a choice, or a positive or negative appreciation or preference,

---

[2] This characterisation is inconsistent with some views about the nature of values. E.g., Jonathan Dancy (in *Moral Reasons*, Oxford: Blackwell, 1993) denies that there are any exceptionless good- (or bad-) making properties. I have argued against his view in *Engaging Reason* (Oxford: Oxford University Press, 2000), chapter 10.

intelligible or justified, is an evaluative property.[3] Comfort or convenience are values, and not only freedom and happiness. Moreover, we do not have abstract nouns naming many evaluative properties, but such properties will be within the scope of this inquiry as well. For example, the thrill of watching a taut and well-executed action film is a value, as the notion is here understood.

This 'inflationary' use of 'value' is not to be judged by linguistic propriety, but by its theoretical purpose, which will emerge as the argument develops, a purpose which in turn is to

---

[3] Some additional clarifications: (a) evaluative properties include those which make the object less rather than more valuable. To simplify, I will normally refer only to positive evaluative properties, but most points apply, with the obvious changes, to both. (b) The characterisation is not meant to be a definition, if by that one means some sort of a canonical explanation of the concept. It is merely a way to enable people with normal command of the language to pick out what is meant. (c) What is meant by 'in itself' in this characterisation is of course as important as it is obscure. I mean to exclude properties whose sole contribution to the value of their possessor is that possession of them is associated, in the context, with others which endow their object with value. For example, that a substance is water is normally associated with the property of being capable of quenching thirst, which makes it good, for it can be used to alleviate the discomfort that thirst involves. But of these properties it is only the capacity to alleviate discomfort which in itself endows water with value. The other properties do so only by their association with it (or some other evaluative property). (d) The characterisation is meant to be consistent with the fact that values can furnish reasons only conditionally: that a chair is comfortable increases its value, even though it is a reason to sit on it only if one has a reason to sit down in the first place. (e) Finally, properties are evaluative even though their 'evaluative' aspect depends on some background conditions of normality, e.g., most values would lose their point if the world were about to end in five minutes. But that does not show that they are not values.

44

govern the elucidation of the contours of the notion beyond the vague characterisation given here by way of initial clarification. At least this much is clear already: the aim is to characterise a category of properties for which we do not have a ready name. Philosophers sometimes talk of the category of the good to capture it, or simply of evaluative properties, both being stipulated uses of these terms. Moreover, they are sometimes used in a narrower way to distinguish some value properties from others, for example, to distinguish them from the virtues, or from deontic properties, which are taken to be outside the good, or the evaluative. For the purposes of the present discussion we need an all-embracing notion of value properties.[4]

[4] The discussion in the previous chapter has illustrated how 'inflationary' my use of 'value' is. It also illustrated some of the considerations which militate in favour of this way of understanding value. It is forced on anyone who thinks that a relationship is certain to be unique in his life (even if unique only in fact). That thought shows that the value of the relationship differs, however subtly, from the value of any other relationship it is at least in fact possible for him or her to have. It amounts to asserting the existence of a complex but distinctive good-making property.

An interesting question is whether values can be unique, in the sense that it is in principle possible for only one object to instantiate them. Some versions of moral particularism, especially those sometimes called situation ethics, say yes, all moral values are unique: what makes a situation such that a certain action is best for an agent in it is a product of everything pertaining to that situation in all its particularity. (There are epistemic versions of this where it is merely that we cannot know which feature makes it such that one response or another is required.) Therefore, there is no general property which makes it such that a particular response is appropriate (the epistemic version merely says that we cannot know what it is). But the possibility of unique evaluative properties can be acknowledged by non-particularists as well.

45

The thesis

The claim that values are universal is, of course, an ancient and familiar one. It has been as often controverted as asserted over the centuries. What does it mean? The thesis to be argued for here cannot claim to be faithful to all the historically important theses about the universality of values. It does, however, capture at least one important motivation for them, and that motivation dictates its scope and nature. We will come to the motivation later. To start with, let us state the thesis simply as:

> *All values are either universal or subsumable under universal values.*

One value is subsumable under another if the only reason why it is a good-making property is that necessarily possession of it instantiates possession of another, more general property, which is a good-making property, and whose possession provides a normatively complete explanation as to why the subsumed property is good-making. [5]

---

[5] The notion of 'a normatively complete explanation' may mislead. I believe that the conditions for the adequacy of any explanation are a function of its purpose and its context. There are no canonically ideal explanations, and no final explanations, i.e., ones such that those who understand them cannot (logically cannot) legitimately request further explanations. However, among adequate explanations, that is, explanations which are true and reasonably meet the needs of context and purpose, some can be said to be normatively complete in the following sense: an explanation is normatively complete if the only requests for further explanations and clarifications regarding its normative adequacy relate to the truth of its normative or evaluative

The core argument: value and intelligibility

The universality of values, I will argue, is an aspect of their intelligibility. To start with what I hope is an intuitive explanation of the argument, imagine that a friend says of a film: 'Today it is a very good film.' Slightly puzzled, I ask, 'And what was it yesterday?' 'Oh', she replies, 'Yesterday it was terrible, very bad indeed.' Now mystified, I ask, 'Do you mean that the film (vehicle on which the film is recorded) has deteriorated suddenly, or that a massacre occurred which makes it impossible for us to enjoy the jokes about massacres in the film?' 'Why should you think that anything must have happened?' replies my friend, 'Nothing of relevance has happened. It is just that the film is no longer a good one, in fact now it is very bad.' At this point I am at a loss to understand what I was told. It cannot be that something will lose or acquire value (i.e., possession of a good- or bad-making property) unless something happened which can explain the change.

This dialogue helps us make two points: first, we believe that we are entitled to assume that any change in value, and similar examples will show the assumption extending to any evaluative state, can be explained. That is, we believe *a priori* that there is an explanation of what is good about good objects or states or events, and of what, when they change their character, accounts for any change in their value. Second, value explanations depend on universal characteristics. Value differences are arbitrary and inexplicable if they are due merely to

premises, that is, if in so far as its adequacy depends on its evaluative propositions it would not be doubted by anyone who understands it and believes in the truth of its normative propositions.

a difference in time or location, or any other aspect of a situation which can only be picked out by singular reference. That of two things one is here rather than there, that it belongs to John rather than to Jane, cannot explain differences in their value. Nor can the fact that of two events one happens today rather than yesterday. Non-universal differences cannot explain evaluative differences between things or events. Not all universal differences make a difference in value intelligible, but only universal features can make it intelligible. The universality of value is, according to this argument, an aspect of the fact that the domain of the evaluative is intelligible through and through, that is, to repeat, that the evaluative character of objects, events, states, and their like can always be explained.

Arguably, we are not entitled to take for granted that there are explanations of why non-evaluative events happen, or of why things are as they are, in the way we are entitled to believe that there are explanations of evaluative events or states. Arguably, within non-evaluative domains we should be willing in principle to accept that facts or events just are as they are, and nothing can explain why they are so. We, perhaps justifiably, believe that we understand large areas of the natural world, and this understanding gives us ground to expect that explanations of events and states within the well-understood domains are forthcoming. However, we may be wrong even there. Besides, in some domains our current knowledge does not justify the assumption that all changes can be explained.[6] Whether or not belief in the availability of an explanation is

---

[6] Whether or not it is always sensible to proceed on a working assumption that all changes can be explained is a different question.

justified seems, when the explained is a non-evaluative event or state, to be an empirical question.

If this difference exists, that is if we can know *a priori* that there are explanations of evaluative events and states, whereas we have no such knowledge of the availability of explanations of non-evaluative states and events, then this is a result of the special character of evaluative explanations. But it must also bear on the ontological properties and status of evaluative properties: they are capable of being understood, and of being explained.[7] There are evaluative explanations of evaluative states and events. Not only can we explain how the film was made, how the money was raised, the camera controlled, the actors directed, etc. We can also explain what it is about it which makes it good or bad, in the ways in which it is good or bad. We can make its value transparent to us, intelligible to us, and do so by providing non-reductive evaluative explanations of its evaluative qualities.

---

[7] It may be thought that the second condition, that they can be explained, goes further than the first, that they can be understood. But this is not altogether clear. The claim that the evaluative can be explained implies, of course, that there are adequate explanations which can be understood by intelligent creatures. Can something be understood without an explanation of it being available? It may be thought that this must be so, for understanding does not imply ability to articulate it in words. But it does not follow from the fact that I can understand what I cannot explain that what I cannot explain cannot be explained. Moreover, the explanation may be consistent with what we normally mean when we say that we cannot articulate what we understand. It may consist in little more than saying: it is like this, and pointing to an analogous phenomenon, for example. This may help people understand what they did not understand before. Of course it presupposes that they already understand a good deal. But that is generally true of most explanations.

Even when we can explain non-evaluative phenomena, we may not be able to explain why the laws of nature, or the causal mechanisms which are relied on in the explanations, are as they are. We can take things one step further: not only do we accept that there may be no explanation of the laws of nature, or the causal mechanisms which explain changes in the world, we also do not understand what it would be to explain all of them. Some laws and mechanisms may be instances of more general ones. But not all laws and causal mechanisms can be instances of more abstract ones. At some point one reaches a bottom line. These just are the laws of nature, and there is no 'why?' about it. The question does not make sense for we do not believe that there is anything which could count as an answer to it.

Not so with evaluative matters. Regarding any good-making property, of the kind we use to explain why things are good or bad and in what ways or to what degree, it is always possible to ask whether it really is a good-making property? What makes it so? Why is it so? Etc. These questions are always in order, and there are true answers to all of them (though, of course, we do not always know them). Value is rational, or intelligible through and through. There are no brute evaluative facts, no 'this is just how things are', as there are, or at least can be, brute non-evaluative facts.

One thought which sometimes generates resistance to this view is a leftover from axiomatic models of explanation. It may take the following form: seemingly, to understand something one needs an explanation of it. An explanation, however, presupposes that its addressee can understand it, and is no use otherwise. Does this lead to a vicious circle? No, for we know that we can understand what we cannot explain. Understanding comes first, and all explanations presuppose it. Therefore, not everything that can be understood can be explained.

This is a fallacious argument. It assumes a linear progression from understanding to explanation to further understanding to further explanations, etc. Nothing in this thought is sound. It may be motivated by a worry about how it all started. How do we understand the first explanation offered to us if we do not have understanding not based on any explanation, and incapable of any explanation. To this the answer (speculative, but reasonable) is that we move in tandem from imperfect understanding and not completely understood explanations to better understanding and better understood explanations. No claim is made that we acquire understanding only through explanations. Only that the question of what comes first is misconceived for it ignores the fact that possibly nothing comes first. It asks where do we get the (adequate) understanding to comprehend and benefit from the first explanation. To which the answer is that (most likely) we do not have it. Most likely we only dimly understood the first explanation, but that may have been enough to get us to improve our understanding a bit, and we went on from there. It is equally possible that we had no understanding (of the relevant kind)[8] prior to encountering the first explanation, and it helped us to acquire a glimmer of understanding, and we went on from there. Philosophically the important point is that while explanation and understanding are interdependent, and one improves the other (or the ability to have the other), there is no strict epistemic priority between

---

[8] For obviously we had an understanding of something.

them, that is, it is not the case that we need to have understanding of something which cannot be explained to understand the explanation of anything.

This may give rise to another worry: is it not the case that there are some explanations which cannot explain, for if you need them you do not understand enough to understand them, and if you are capable of understanding them you do not need them, they do not *explain* anything you did not understand before. If so, it is at best misleading to call them explanations just because they take the form that explanations often take. To illustrate the point, imagine that someone asks:

> Q. What is bad in taking pleasure in making others suffer?

Some think that the wrongness of taking pleasure in making others suffer is a brute or ultimate moral fact, which admits of no explanation. But I think that the following is an explanatory reply:

> E. In taking pleasure in the suffering of others one is
> displaying insensitivity to their suffering, and a lack of
> concern for it, which is particularly reprehensible if one is
> oneself the cause of the suffering, and could have
> prevented it.

I would not claim that this is the only explanation possible, or the most appropriate one, only that depending on what puzzled the inquirer it may be an adequate explanation. But, is it not the case that if the inquirer does not already know the answer to his question the explanation will not help him? He will remain unconvinced. There is, the objection goes, nothing we can say to explain to him why taking pleasure in making others suffer is bad.

The plausibility of the objection depends on a simple-minded view of failures of understanding, which are often failures to connect. When the connection appears very obvious it may seem that one could not fail to be mindful of it. But this is not so. Even very simple connections can escape one, and explanations can be in principle helpful to draw attention to them. A further objection to the availability of explanations may now suggest itself: am I assuming that it is always possible to convince anyone who is willing to listen and consider explanations seriously? This is implausible and once we reject that assumption we must reject the availability of explanations. This objection is, however, misconceived. The availability of explanations does not guarantee the possibility of persuasion even of a patient and rational inquirer. Such inquirers may have different beliefs, or different epistemic profiles which will make it impossible to convince them of their error. Intelligibility of value does not guarantee convergence of all rational inquirers.[9]

That value should be intelligible in that way is of course no empirical discovery. Rather, it is of the nature of the evaluative that it is intelligible, and it is part of the function of that part of our conceptual ability to show that it lends itself to our understanding. We can ask of course how could it be so? How is it that explanations are always forthcoming? But that is not a question which can be pursued here. All that remains for our purpose is to point out that the intelligibility of value

---

[9] I have examined some of the reasons for this failure in chapter 6 of *Engaging Reason.*

presupposes the universality of the concepts used in the explanation. That was the burden of the example of the film allegedly changing in quality from one day to the other. It illustrates the point that intelligibility presupposes universality.

2 When are values universal?

In stating the thesis and explaining the argument for it I relied on our existing understanding of universality. When, however, we try to articulate that understanding we find that we entertain conflicting views about the meaning of the thesis of the universality of value.

I believe that the following two conditions come close to capturing our notion of universal properties: an evaluative property is universal if and only if:

1 The conditions for its application can be stated without use of singular references, that is, without any reference to place or time, or to any named individual, etc.
2 In principle, it can be instantiated in any place and at any time.

The second condition is meant to cover cases where, while the good-making property can be specified without reference to any particulars, its nature is such that it can only be instantiated at certain times, or before or after a certain time, etc. I am not sure whether there are such cases, but their exclusion seems part of our notion of universality (or of one of them).

The problem is that while the two conditions seem to explain our notion of the universality of properties in general, they do not capture what we understand by claims that

54

values are universal. The two conditions allow for differentiations between many classes of people which are inconsistent with assertions about the universality of values, as commonly understood.

A few examples will help to show how far the two conditions I stated in themselves fail to satisfy our intuitive notion of a universal value:

- Not all temporal references are excluded by the two conditions. For example: a property which applies only to all fifty-year-old people, or one which applies only to all children, meets the conditions, and if they are sufficient for universality such properties are universal properties. Though properties which necessarily apply only to those born within fifty years of the bombing of Hiroshima, or ones which necessarily apply only to all those living in Ipswich, are not universal.
- Properties which apply only to men or only to women, for example, manly virtues, or feminine virtues, understood as virtues which only men or women can possess, are, by the two criteria I stated, universal properties. So are racial properties, virtues which only whites can possess, for example. Though, interestingly, ethnic properties are not universal. Virtues that only Russians can possess fail the test of universality.
- 'Born in London' is a non-universal condition, but 'born in a city with more than eight million inhabitants' is universal.

Normally none of these counts as a universal property, or condition. Gender-based, or race-based, properties seem to us to offend against universality just as much as ethnic properties do. Allowing the former while excluding the latter strikes us as arbitrary.

Am I not making a mistake in the way I drew the distinction? This is not a question of linguistic propriety. There is plenty of precedent for the use of 'universal' in accordance with the characterisation offered here, as well as for other ways of demarcating its boundaries. The question is of the grounds for the distinction and its purposes. For example, those who talk of universal human rights may have in mind something like 'rights which are possessed by all human beings'. That would exclude the rights of males or of those born in very large cities from counting as universal.

Perhaps the problem is solved by adding a third condition of universality:

3. A value is universal only if, if at least some people can display it, then it is in principle possible for every individual person to display it. Put in other words: it is in principle possible for every individual person to display all the universal values that any person can display.

This is meant to allow for cat virtues, that is, virtues which only cats can possess, etc. It insists, however, on people's universal accessibility, in some weak sense, to human values. That is, the condition does not apply to evaluative properties which no humans can possess at all, properties which can be instantiated only by landscapes, or planets, or plants. If a property can be instantiated by people, however, the condition determines that it is universal only if in principle any person can possess it.

Does the third condition succeed in capturing our intuitive understanding of universal values? I do not think that it does. Even according to it, values can be universal and yet very specific. A condition for holding a right may be that one is the first student of the youngest university, provided that no other university has been established within ten years before it. Very few people ever qualify to hold such a right. Value properties can be both universal and specific to such a degree that given how the world is, no more than one particular can instantiate them. Why, given this fact, does it matter whether values are all universal or whether some of them are particular? The answer is that the common understanding of universal values draws no such distinction. According to it, highly specific values of this kind are not universal. But if so then the third condition does not capture the common notion of the universality of values.

These doubts are reinforced by examining the third condition directly. It stated that a value property which can be possessed by some person is universal only if it can be possessed by any person. This was meant to capture, among other things, our common understanding of universality, an understanding which denies that value properties which are specific to members of one gender or one race are universal properties. But does the condition do justice to our views on this point?

It is possible for some people to change gender. Suppose that it is, or will become, possible for everyone to change gender. Would that show that gender-specific value properties are universal? Our unarticulated understanding of the notion disagrees. It may be possible in principle, or logically possible, for everyone to change gender, but in fact it is impossible for most people to do so. Sex change was in fact impossible for all those who lived before the procedures for it were developed, and it remains *de facto* impossible for most people living today. Therefore, gender-specific values are not universal, by the common understanding of universal values. Take another example. Suppose that some value property can be possessed only by members of a hereditary aristocracy (whose members descend in the right way from people who were ennobled by a once-elected king or queen). It is possible for anyone to possess these properties, for the monarch can ennoble anyone. But such properties are hardly universal value properties.

Clearly the common understanding of 'universal values' insists on more than the formal possibility that every person may possess the evaluative property in question. Does the common notion of universal rights and values insist that only rights and values which everyone enjoys, not merely ones which everyone can in principle enjoy, are universal? Not everyone is funny or amusing, but we are, I assume, happy to regard this as a universal evaluative property.

At this point I am inclined to give up. I doubt that any formal condition can be found which will successfully articulate our intuitive understanding of universal values. The view that values are universal, as a commonly expressed view, seems to me to be a *substantive moral view*. It is not a view about the nature of value, or of any other evaluative concept. It is a product of the moral struggle for the rejection of certain false value distinctions: the rejection of the special privileges of the aristocracy, and the evaluative beliefs which underpinned them in pre-enlightenment Europe, the rejection of racism and sexism, and the like. The insistence on universality *in that elusive sense* was a product of the attempt to show that to the extent that belief in such values encapsulates any truth at all, this is because they are subsumed under others, which people came to think of as 'truly universal' values.[10]

Needless to say, we should embrace that rejection (of 'aristocratic', sexist, or racist, etc., values) or those efforts towards their subsumption. But we mislead ourselves if we think that they generalise beyond the unmasking of particular false evaluative beliefs. We mislead ourselves if we think that the unmasking was done by bringing to light a general feature of all values or all moral values, namely their universality. The truth seems to be that things are the other way round: the only way we can understand what we mean when we assert the universality of value is by reference to the rejection of those false values about which rage past or present moral struggles, and other false values like them, that is, other false values intuitively understood to be sufficiently like them.

This means, of course, that *the commonly understood view* that values are universal is without theoretical interest. It can teach us something about the history of moral debates in the West, but it can teach us nothing about the nature of value or of morality.

3 The reversal argument

In giving up on the significance of *the common view* about the universality of value I do not mean to abandon the

---

[10] For by extension we call 'universal' values which are not themselves universal but are subsumable under ones which are.

thesis altogether. I will understand the thesis to relate to universality understood in accordance with the first two conditions I stated above. Evaluative properties are universal if the conditions of their instantiation can be stated without singular reference and if they can be instantiated in any place or time. Thus understood, the thesis is true and of importance. It is a consequence of the fact that the domain of the evaluative is essentially intelligible.

As we saw that thesis, the theoretical thesis, as I will call it, is much weaker, less demanding, than the common belief in the universality of values. Nevertheless, even it is threatened by arguments relying on the theoretical significance of the diversity in our value beliefs and practices. There are various attempts to argue from diversity to the rejection of the universality of value. I will set out and discuss only one such argument. I will call it *the reversal argument* for it starts with a familiar sceptical argument from social diversity and reverses it to establish the possibility of evaluative knowledge, but at the cost of abandoning the universality of value – or so the argument runs.

The first stage: the argument from social diversity

One of the oldest arguments in the book is that values cannot be objective because they vary from place to place and from time to time. One can debate the degree of diversity we actually witness. Some have claimed that the diversity is of different ways of pursuing the same values – implying that by and large they are all acceptable. However, I will not follow that path and will accept for the sake of the argument that there is significant diversity in values, or in people's beliefs about values.

What does the argument from diversity show? Perhaps all it shows is that people make mistakes? The problem is that it seems inexplicable why so many people should make so many mistakes. It is more plausible to think that they diverge because there is nothing for them to know, or at least nothing that they can know. Others respond by trying to explain the causes of the divergence: perhaps there is growth and development in our (the human race's) ability to understand values and to conform to them, etc. I will consider neither the claim nor the attempts at its rebuttal, for the argument from diversity should not, I believe, be taken to rest on these empirical claims. Rather it consists of two premises

(a) To attribute knowledge in any domain we must be in a position to explain how knowledge can be acquired and how mistakes can be made.

(b) The explanation of the possibility of knowledge must show how we can be sensitive to what we know, how, in forming and holding beliefs in the domain, we are sensitive to the way things are regarding the matters our beliefs are about. The explanation of the possibility of error must explain how we can fail to be adequately sensitive.

The argument from diversity claims that we fail this test regarding values. Our beliefs about values are sensitive to the social practices around us, sensitive to the views we encounter in our life. They are not sensitive to how things really are regarding values. Hence, either there are no values, or we can know nothing about them.

Reversing the argument

It happens to many arguments that they can be turned on their head. After all, all an argument establishes is that it cannot be that the premises are true and the conclusion is false. Arguments are presented in the form: since the premises are true so is the conclusion. But they can be turned on their head to show that since the conclusion is false so is the premise. A similar fate can befall the argument from diversity. But the reversal I have in mind here is not the straightforward reversal of rejecting the premises because one rejects the conclusion. Rather, instead of arguing that since values depend on society they cannot be objective, the reversal argument that I will examine makes a more paradoxical claim: since values are objective, they cannot be independent of social conditions.

Let us examine this a little: as I said, this is not the simple reversal of denying that values depend on social conditions. I am not going to challenge the social dependence of value.[11] Nor will I challenge what is – for our argument – the basic fact, that is, the fact of diversity. Yet the reversal argument rejects the conclusion, for it, the reversal argument, is

---

[11] Nor do I mean to endorse it here. The reversal argument depends on some form of social dependence obtaining. Where it does not obtain the argument does not hold, at least not in the form presented here, and the possibility of knowledge depends on some other facts. I'll return to this point below.

based on the equally firmly held belief in the objectivity of value, and in the possibility of evaluative knowledge. Given that, value's dependence on the social is turned to advantage: it provides the way in which the reversal argument is going to meet the lesson we learnt, that is, that the claim of the possibility of knowledge within a domain must be capable of being backed by an explanation of how people's beliefs about matters within the domain can be sensitive to the way things are within it.

The sceptical argument takes the fact of diversity as good evidence to suppose that belief in value is socially conditioned. It therefore draws the conclusion that belief in value cannot be sensitive to value. We do not learn to believe that this or that is of value from the fact that it is of value, nor that something else is without value from the fact that it is without value. We acquire our beliefs from our society.[12] This shows that belief in value is not objective. That is, either there are no values, or we cannot know anything about them.

The reversal argument starts by rejecting the conclusion and accepting the objectivity of values, and the possibility of knowledge about value. Hence, it concludes, to the extent that knowledge of them is sensitive to social practices, and given the lesson that knowledge must be explained by sensitivity to

---

[12] The argument does not assume that we simply come to accept beliefs which are prevalent around us. All it supposes is that the explanation of why we believe what we believe turns on the beliefs we find around us. Their influence can take any shape or form, including reacting against it and rejecting society's views. This also means that the argument does not assume unanimity of belief in the society we live in or grow up in.

what is known, it follows that values themselves depend on social practices.

Dependence through creation and access

To be capable of explaining how knowledge of value is possible, the dependence of values on the social must be relatively strong. Much has been written in recent years about the truism that concepts are historical products, emerging or created at particular times or particular periods in the course of history. But the relevance of this point in itself is unclear. It may show that people did not know, and perhaps even could not have known, of some values before some concepts emerged which enabled them to form beliefs about these values. Even this conclusion cannot be established without further premises.

To see the point, consider the case of simple sensual pleasures, such as the pleasure people take in their favourite colours, or tastes, or pleasures in certain sensations of movement, of the kind that many very young children enjoy spontaneously, and which form the basis of some fairground attractions. Such pleasures are intrinsically good, and their value has probably been known to people ever since their sense organs, brains, and nervous system took roughly the shape they have today. It is possible that some social training is relevant even for the capacity to enjoy these pleasures. But there is no reason to think that they were ever unavailable to people whose constitution enabled them to enjoy such pleasures. True, the concept of sensual pleasures is a historical–social product. But it is plausible to think that people always knew about these pleasures, that is, that they knew of them before they had this concept. They had some other ways of referring to them, and they may have been able to experience them, or at any rate some of them, even when they could not have known about them, could not have had beliefs about them at all.

The example of sensual pleasures reminds us that any sensible thesis about the social dependence of values will be limited. There are values, such as sensual pleasures, whose social dependence is minimal. This may not matter. Precisely because the ability to enjoy them is not socially dependent, they are immune to the sceptical argument from diversity, and we do not need to rely on the reversal argument to vindicate their objectivity, and the possibility of knowledge about them.[13]

Still, generally speaking,[14] to entertain thoughts and to have beliefs we need concepts, and as concepts are historical products so is the ability to have the beliefs and thoughts which they are needed for. In that way, at least in that way,

---

[13] There may, of course, be a diversity of views about whether pleasure is valuable, and whether it is so conditionally or unconditionally, whether only some pleasures are valuable, and how those which are valuable relate to other goods. But these are largely theoretical debates. Theoretical disputes and disagreements do not lead as easily to sceptical conclusions as do disagreements about what is valuable.

[14] This qualification is meant to allow for pre- (or non-) conceptual thoughts or beliefs, and for the possibility that it may be right to attribute thoughts and beliefs, statement of which requires concepts, to people who do not have those concepts. I think that even if one should allow for these possibilities the following remarks are unaffected, though they may have to be more carefully stated.

the possibility of some knowledge about evaluative matters is historically conditioned, not only in presupposing possession of some appropriate concepts, but in that those concepts were not always available. Such concepts emerged at some time in history, and made possible thoughts, beliefs, and knowledge which was unavailable before their emergence.

The ability of individuals to 'invent' concepts does not avoid the dependence of concepts on the social. To 'invent' a concept one would need an array of other concepts for that invention. No one can invent all the concepts needed for further invention, and therefore everyone depends on socially available concepts to think about and to understand values.

But that in itself does not show that values, as against thinking and entertaining beliefs about them, are socially dependent in any way. The dependence of thought about values on culture would not, without further premises, show that the sensitivity of our beliefs about value to culture constitutes, or can under some conditions constitute, sensitivity to the reality of value, which is what we need to show to establish the possibility of knowledge of value.

What would one need to show in order to establish that in being socially dependent our beliefs about value can be sensitive to the reality of value? It would be enough to show that the very existence of the value is socially dependent (and in a way which correlates with the way our beliefs are socially dependent). Regarding many values arguments to that effect may be forthcoming.

Take the game of chess. It was invented, or developed, at a certain time. It is a historical product. Or think of opera. It too is a more or less datable historical product. They brought with them new forms of excellence, new goods. There are several of them. Think, for the purpose of the current argument, of two: excellence in playing chess (or in chess openings, etc.) and in singing in operas, excellence as an opera singer (or as a dramatic soprano, etc.). There were no opera singers, nor chess players, before the emergence of opera and chess, nor could there have been. *A fortiori* there were no excellent opera singers or chess players. That form of excellence could not be manifested before opera and chess came to be. Did it exist before them? Did the good or form of excellence pre-date the possibility of its manifestation? It seems plausible to deny that, plausible to think that the goods which are bound up with chess and opera (and which in part make them what they are) came into being with chess and opera. To argue for that would take us into rarefied and arcane aspects of ontology which may not be directly relevant to the soundness of the reversal argument.

To see that, let us take another example: that of friendship, which can here represent the good of any interpersonal relationship. It is like chess and opera in that they all are instances of (intrinsic) goods engagement with which presupposes at least some understanding of their nature. Most intrinsic values require a degree of intellectual or cognitive engagement. Playing any game requires knowledge of the game it is, engaging in cultural activities benefits one only if done with understanding, and that requires understanding of the kind of cultural activity one is engaged in: is one reading a novel or a poem, listening to an opera, or to a pop song, etc.? Friendship requires knowledge of how relating to a friend differs from relating to other people, etc.[15]

It seems to me that if the reversal argument works for the forms of the good constitutive of the nature of chess and of opera it also applies to the good of friendship, or the goods, virtues, etc., which are inseparable from it. However, it does not feel quite right to say that the virtue of being a good friend came into being at the time, in early human history, when friendship became possible.[16] It may be that it is possible to talk of the emergence of new values more comfortably when they are associated with easily identifiable social institutions: chess, opera, or the state (whose emergence generates ideals of good citizenship), or the law (with its special virtues such as the rule of law, etc.). It is odd to talk of the value of friendship, or

[15] Some are inclined to deny that friendship depends on knowledge of what is and what is not appropriate between friends. They regard that supposition as a legalistic, rule-dependent conception (or misconception) of friendship, which they believe to be a condition arising out of natural feeling towards the friend. That involves both the confusion of social meaning with legal-type rules, and the mistake of thinking that 'natural' un-socially-tutored feelings towards another are sufficient for friendship. Of course, a liking of one's friend is common among friends, and essential to many friendships. But the relationship becomes friendship only when those feelings are framed in ways which are learnt through one's socialisation and when they fit, however awkwardly and with however many individual variations, into the common understanding of friendship.
[16] It is possible that some form of sociability emerged with the very emergence of *homo sapiens*. If so, its development into some form of friendship as we know it from human history went hand in hand with the development of language and of the more complex social norms it makes possible.

love, or courage as emerging at a particular time. Sociologists and historians do so, but philosophers tend to accuse them of confusion between belief in these values, or belief in the particular form they took in different countries and periods, and the values themselves.

Possibly there is no point, no content to propositions about the existence of values, forms of the good, virtue, and their like. Possibly, some or all are a-temporal, and possibly some or all have existence in time. Whatever the proper view of these matters, the reversal argument does not depend on it. In chapter 4 I will argue that values are realised only when people (or other creatures) successfully engage in them. By their nature, values and goods are capable of being engaged with,[17] and, in a loose sense, being realised through people engaging with them is the point of their existence. If they exist prior to the time when the conditions for their realisation obtain that is a shadowy existence, a shadow cast by our grammar. After all values can have no effect in the world except through being recognised, and no proper effect except through being engaged with in the appropriate way. Hence, all the reversal argument need do is to show that where the possibility of engaging with values is socially dependent it is so in a way which takes the sting out of the fact that belief in values is socially dependent.

Regarding any intrinsic value, if one could show that, first, engagement with it presupposes some understanding of its nature; and second, that such an understanding is not possible without mastery of socially dependent concepts, one would be well on the way towards an argument establishing the social

---

[17] I have advanced some arguments to that effect in *Engaging Reason*.

dependence of value. As I said, regarding many intrinsic values arguments of this general shape are available.

Two sample objections to the reversal argument

The reversal argument may appear too quick. It can be charged that it assumes:

a. that value beliefs and practices are uniform throughout any given society or cultural group; and
b. that the way people's value practices depend on social practices is always by imitation, by joining in.

If one rejects these assumptions, the objections allege, it is impossible to reverse the sceptical argument. There just are too many incompatible value practices within a country to make sense of the claim that they each encapsulate values. Similarly, in developing their evaluative views people often rebel against prevailing opinion. When they do so they may go in many directions. For any value dogma there are many alternatives and those who rebel against the dogma react in different ways. Again, it is impossible to think that value tracks all these reactions. The reversal argument leads not to some stable social dependence of value, but to an incoherent and chaotic account, which is bound to collapse into value subjectivism, namely that each person is bound by his/her own beliefs and nothing else – a position which is clearly false and in most versions incoherent.

Reply: the objections draw attention to important points. They remind us of familiar facts with which any account of the social dependence of value must be compatible. But it is not clear that they condemn the social dependence thesis outright.

After all, not all social practices encapsulate value. This was never the claim. All that the objection shows is that the determination of which practices do and which do not must be sensitive to the points raised by it. Is there any general reason to think that this cannot be so? There is if one intends to characterise social practices in non-evaluative terms only, and then, relying on such a description, expect to be able to pick out which practices encapsulate goods, which bads, and which neither. That is a hopeless task. But all that that shows is what we knew, or should have known, all along, namely, that it is impossible to give reductive explanations of the evaluative phenomena.

The thesis that many intrinsic values depend on social practices does not presuppose a reductive account of values. It allows that the description and explanation of the social practices which generate values are themselves evaluative. Once this is allowed we have no reason to believe that the two objections raise concerns which cannot be met. To be confident that they can be successfully met we must await a better understanding of the way intrinsic values depend on the social, to the extent that they do. Meantime, we can provisionally accept the reversal argument as a powerful argument for the dependence of some intrinsic values on the social.

From social sensitivity to particularism

The argument also appears to have a direct consequence for the question we are investigating. Namely, it seems to yield a proof of particularism. If value is socially dependent, it follows that values vary with social facts, and these social facts are mere contingent facts. They are there today, gone tomorrow. And so it is, it would seem, with values. They are here today and are gone tomorrow.

Must this violate the universality of values? Suppose we think only of those values regarding which the case for their temporality, the case for their creation or emergence in time, is strongest. It may be thought that at least in their case the social dependence of value establishes the temporality of values, and therefore their particularity. But that turns out to be a complex matter. I think that it is fair to say that a common understanding of what is meant by assertions that 'values are universal' takes it to imply that they are either eternal or a-temporal, or at least co-terminous with the existence of the world or perhaps with the existence of human beings. Perhaps it is even right that that is the dominant understanding of the claim that values are universal. It is much less clear whether the temporality of values would violate the two conditions of universality I set out above.

The first condition is clearly not necessarily violated by temporal values. Their temporality does not make it necessary in spelling out their content to refer to any particulars. Is the second condition violated? It stipulates that to be universal a value must be capable of being instantiated at any time. Clearly it cannot be instantiated when it does not exist, but is it not enough for it to be possible that it is instantiated at time t that it is possible for it to exist at t (and that there is nothing else which prevents its instantiation)? If so, then the second condition is not violated by the temporality of values as such. That they do not exist at a certain time does not show that it would have been impossible for them then to exist. Nor is there anything in the social-dependence thesis to suggest otherwise. There is no reason to think that the social developments which led to the concepts on which the existence of the value depends could not have emerged before, or that other concepts enabling the value to come into existence could not have emerged at an earlier time.[18]

You can test these abstract points by considering again some typical intrinsic values, such as the value of being a friend, or of listening to opera, or of playing chess. Friendship, opera, and chess are social creations, and therefore they are goods which came into being at some point or period in time, and did not exist before that, in the sense that there were no friendships, operas, or chess games before a certain time. Assume that the values which can be realised only in friendship, chess, or opera, goods which can be manifested only through them, could not have existed before that time either. Nevertheless, these goods are universal, for they can in principle be instantiated at any point in time or space (and would have been so instantiated had the proper social conditions existed earlier), and the conditions for their instantiation do not involve necessary use of singular reference.

Contingent particularity?

The social dependence of value does not make it necessary that values are not universal. But is it not the case that it makes their particularity possible? Some may claim that it is quite likely to lead to the conclusion that we should admit

---

[18] The conditions elaborated in chapter 10 of *Engaging Reason* seem to me to conform with the common notion of universality while allowing for a temporal dimension to values.

particularity of some values, though this again depends on what precisely we mean by universality.

These matters are more complex than can be sorted out here. I will conclude with two remarks. First, we can rely at this juncture on the argument from the intelligibility of value. The intelligibility of value requires its universality. The social dependence of value does not require that it not be universal. Should we not conclude that the two are reconcilable and that necessarily value is both intelligible, and therefore universal, and socially dependent?

Nothing I said is sufficiently solid to warrant that conclusion. But my discussion may nonetheless be helpful in pointing out that what appear to be irreconcilable conflicts, namely the conflicts between diversity and universality of value, and between the social dependence of value and its intelligibility, are not in fact irreconcilable conflicts. I do not pretend to have done enough to establish the right way to reconcile them. But I hope I have done enough to show that reconciliation is possible.

However, my final remark has to be that in my central assumption I may have over-generalised. My central assumption was that the evaluative domain is intelligible, and that its intelligibility is non-reductive: we can understand what is of value and what makes it so, and our understanding rests on the availability of evaluative explanations of all evaluative phenomena.

Perhaps, however, that intelligibility is in some ways only partial? There is reason to believe that to be so.[19] For

---

[19] It is partial in other respects as well: there is no guarantee that we can explain why something good or bad came to pass, only what it is about

example, we know that while our reasons for our actions make our actions intelligible to us, they do so only incompletely. Let me briefly explain: our actions are our own only if we act for reasons, and our reasons are those aspects of the action and its circumstances which made the action eligible to us.[20] We may admit in retrospect that we were mistaken, that we acted for the wrong reasons, and even that we acted irrationally, preferring the lesser reason to the stronger ones. So long as we retain the ability to understand our actions as actions for reasons, we retain our ability to understand why we did them, even when we were misguided or irrational to do them. By seeing them as intelligible we can see them as ours.

But not all aspects of our actions are rendered intelligible by reason. We are not Buridan's ass; we can act in the knowledge that the reasons for the action do not make it better than some available alternatives. Here our reasons explain why we did what we did, but they do not explain why we did this rather than the equally eligible alternative. Intelligibility does not extend that far. It does not go all the way.

It is possible that there are similar limitations on our understanding of what is good about good phenomena. There may be an element of brute contingency there too. That will set

what came to pass which makes it good or bad. The rest is a matter for ordinary causal explanations. Can we understand how evaluative properties relate to non-evaluative ones? Perhaps, but the thesis about the intelligibility of value does not guarantee that either.

[20] Actions are not our own, in the sense here assumed, if they are accidental, or manipulated under hypnosis, etc. To avoid misunderstanding I should add that this condition for being our own actions, which is more fully explained in chapter 1 of *Engaging Reason*, does not set the outer limit of actions or events for which we are responsible.

a limit to the intelligibility of value, and therefore perhaps to its universality. The failure is unlikely to falsify the universality thesis, nor to lead to withdrawing the thesis of the intelligibility of values. But it will set limits on them, limits on the degree to which more general concepts explain less general ones: 'This is beautiful because it is harmonious, with a perfect balance of colour and form.' Evaluative explanations normally take some such form: we explain judgements made in more general terms by reference to judgements made in more specific ones. But the relationship between concepts at different levels of generality is not totally perspicacious. Is it necessary that what is harmonious should be beautiful? There are certainly other forms and norms of beauty. Beauty can be based on dissonance, or precariousness and imbalance, and so on.

Could it be a mere historical contingency that clarity is admired under the norms of one style, one form, whereas misty haze is admired by another, that solidity and permanence contribute to one norm of beauty, whereas fluidity and effervescence are the soul of another? If so, then there is an element of pure contingency at the heart of values, a contingency which can be explained historically only, through explanations which lack the element of necessity. This contingency sets limits to the intelligibility of value, and may affect our understanding of the nature of its universality. But these are matters which call for much further reflection.

3

The value of staying alive

1 Framing the question

To anticipate: I will endorse Epicurus' view that 'death is nothing to us',[1] or rather a version of it. My reasons are not his, and do not depend on endorsing the view that only sensations are good or bad. Human life, I will argue, is not intrinsically and unconditionally valuable at all. The ancient doubts about people's life being good for them were many, and my argument will be no more than a variant on some of them. I will use it to argue for the view that life is a precondition of good, and normally a conditional good, but that it is not unconditionally and intrinsically good.[2] I will call this *the thesis*.

The approach underlying the thesis can be described thus: people's life can be of value (or good, or valuable – I will use various expressions as designating roughly the same idea)

---

[1] From his letter to Meneoecus.

[2] I will write interchangeably about things being good and having value, or being valuable. Roughly speaking, something is instrumentally good if it is good because of the value of consequences it will, or may have, or because of the value of consequences it can be used to achieve. Money and tools are instrumentally good in this second way. Taking medication to cure some illness is instrumentally good in the first way. Any good which is not instrumentally good is intrinsically good. This is a rather wide way of conceiving of intrinsic goods. Some intrinsic goods, for example, turn out to be conditional goods. Conditional goods are those which are good because something else is, when the relationship between them is a necessary relationship.

or without value. It can also be bad with negative value only (as well as, of course, bad on balance, i.e. with good and bad, but with the bad predominating). The value of one's life is determined by the value of one's activities, relationships, and experiences, in short, by the value of its content.[3] The value of continuing alive depends upon the value of the content of one's life if one were to remain alive longer. Alternatively, perhaps, it depends on what it is reasonable to expect the content of one's future life to be. The content (or the reasonably antici-pated content) of one's life can be good or bad. Which it is is a contingent matter. Nothing can be derived from it regarding the value of life in and of itself.

Even supporters of the thesis may believe that its truth is a matter of rarefied theoretical interest. How can the distinc-tion between life being good, and it being a precondition of the good, matter in practice (especially since even if it is intrinsi-cally good it may contain bad experiences which make it bad on balance)? I believe that this is mistaken. I think that there is a great resistance to accept the thesis, and not much hope that it will soon become the common view. But were it to be so it would make a real difference to the common perception of questions of life and death. There are of course risks that it or its consequences will be misunderstood, and yield bad results. Were it to be correctly appreciated, however, it might save us many contortious arguments. I will not try to establish this case here. But before entering the debate about the thesis let me give one illustration of its practical importance, derived from the

---

[3] As well as by the way one's life came to have that content (was it choice or necessity, etc.).

case of the Siamese twins, known as Jodie and Mary, in which
the English Court of Appeal had to decide whether to order
(or approve) an operation to separate them which would kill
Mary, or agree with the parents who refused to allow the operation, in which case both would die within a few months. In
considering the interest of Mary, Lord Justice Ward (as quoted
in *The Guardian*), speaking for the court, said:

> Determining where Mary's welfare lies is more difficult.
> The judge found, and I agree, that her state is pitiable and
> will never improve . . . The real issue of difficulty for me
> lies in the judge's finding that the remaining few months of
> her life if not separated would 'be simply worth nothing to
> her, they would be hurtful'. This led him to conclude that
> 'to prolong Mary's life for these few months would be very
> seriously to her disadvantage'.
>
> Whether these remaining months will be hurtful
> or not is not the important question in this case. What is of
> real importance and public interest is the assessment that
> her life is worth nothing . . . The sanctity of life doctrine is
> so enshrined as a fundamental principle of law and
> commands such respect from the law that I am compelled
> to accept that each life has inherent value in itself however
> grave the impairment of some of the body's functions may
> be. I am satisfied that Mary's life, desperate as it is, still has
> its own ineliminable value and dignity. In my judgment
> the learned judge was wrong to find it was worth nothing.
> He also erred in his finding that to prolong Mary's life
> would be seriously to her disadvantage.[4]

---

[4] Re A (Children), quoted from *The Guardian*, Saturday, 23 September
2000.

It is not my claim that Lord Justice Ward was wrong in law. But were the truth of the thesis generally recognised, he would not have been compelled to accept the false view he did accept, and then find a difficult argument to undo its results (for the operation which would kill Mary was approved by the court which found, among other things, that 'Though Mary has a right to life, she has little right to be alive', and judged that the best interest of 'the twins', taken as one entity, would be served by sacrificing Mary's interest to Jodie's). He could have simply relied on the finding about her own best interest. Neither this nor any other illustration is conclusive on the practical difference clear apprehension of the thesis would make. For the rest of this chapter, its truth rather than its practical relevance is all that matters.

The examination of the thesis will proceed as follows. This section will include some further reflections on the nature of the question to be examined here, distinguishing it from other questions, not here taken up. Section 2, by examining three failed arguments for the thesis, will survey some of the complexities surrounding it, especially the way the value of the content of our life is related to our mortality, and the different attitudes it may be reasonable to have towards death. Section 3 will examine the thesis directly. Section 4 will consider whether the desire to remain alive conflicts with the thesis, whereas the concluding section, section 6, does the same for the fear of death. It concludes that while fear of death cannot be generally condemned as irrational, nor does it refute the view here advocated. Before that, in section 5, I defend a key assumption of my argument. It crucially presupposes that we can separate life from its content, that we can judge life not to be intrinsically valuable and maintain that the value of being or staying alive depends on the content of that life, which can make the life good, bad, or indifferent. As against that, one may argue that there is no way of separating life from some (intrinsically valuable) aspects of its content. I will criticise that view in the form it was given by Tom Nagel in section 5.

The value of life and of personal survival

I wanted to talk about the value of life. However, this topic is elusive. On its face it covers (at least some aspects of) such diverse matters as the wrongness of assault and homicide, the absolute prohibition against torture, the way we treat members of other species, the reasons for preserving the species now in existence, the provision of health care, the eradication of hunger and starvation, the wrongness, if any, of suicide, reasons for having children, and for not having more, and much else.

Even if one confines one's attention to the value of *human* life the diversity of concerns often subsumed under that heading is bewildering. It is not easy to see how one value, or one deontic requirement, can account for all of them. The problem is that if we suppose that human life has value, that is, a value attached to any human life, then it is difficult to account for the difference, for example, between the reasons for having more children and the reasons against killing people solely by reference to it. Possibly, the variety of reasons present in these and other cases often thought to exemplify the value of life may not in fact derive just from a single value. To account for the diversity of concerns one may have to invoke a range of different values. If so, what is it that unites all of them as manifesting the value of life?

I will sidestep these doubts and problems by concentrating on one concern, namely the concern for personal survival, for staying alive. In terminology, I will alternate between talking of 'the value of survival', 'the value of continued existence', 'the value of staying alive', and 'the value of life'. None of them is entirely suitable. 'Survival' suggests the presence of threats, and of a struggle. While these are familiar enough, their presence is not essential for the value I will focus on. I will use all these expressions to refer to the value, if any, of a living human being remaining alive at least for a while longer. When using the phrase 'the value of life' nothing more will be meant.

One advantage of posing the question in this way is that it carries no implications as to the value of creating new life. Some people do believe in the value of life in a wider sense. They believe that there is value in creating or bringing about new life. The more the better. I take the claim that survival is valuable to be less controversial. This is why I focus on it.

Another advantage of this way of framing the subject is the distinction it allows between the value of people's past life and that of their survival. It seems possible for me to believe that my life to date was of some value, and yet to believe that my continuing alive is of no value at all. Similarly it seems possible to hold that there has been no value to one's life so far but that this makes it all the more important that one should carry on living: the lack of value in one's past life makes one's survival more valuable. Whether or not such views are ever true, they seem meaningful, and sometimes not without some plausibility. Their possibility does not force us to conclude that the value of people's past life is different in kind from the value of their survival, but it leaves room for that possibility, which I wish to leave open, at least at the beginning.

Another way in which the value of personal survival is narrower than the value of life is that it does not encompass consideration of the value of the life of other animals, nor of the survival of species. I believe that the following discussion is relevant to all these cases, but it does not automatically resolve the questions they give rise to. These will not be touched upon.

Personal and impersonal value of survival

The thesis that life is not of unconditional intrinsic value to the person whose life it is appears on the surface consistent with the supposition that it may have impersonal value. What has (intrinsic) impersonal value is good (*simpliciter*) though not necessarily good for anyone, and certainly not necessarily good for everyone. Yet if their own life is not of value to people there is an apparent paradox in holding that it has impersonal value. In general, whatever is good *simpliciter*, and is not inconsistent with what is good for me on other grounds, is, if I can engage with it in the right way, good for me. So if my life is good *simpliciter* then it would appear that it is not good for me only if it conflicts with what would be otherwise good for me. While we can think of cases where death would be good for one (e.g., if one is in the terminal stages of a painful cancer), this is not generally the case. Therefore, it would seem that if my life is good *simpliciter* it is also good for me, special cases excepted. Or, by counter-position, since it is not good for me it is not good *simpliciter*. This argument assumes, however, that if it is good *simpliciter* then it is a good with which I can engage. Could it be otherwise? Could my life present a value to others which they can relate to in ways which are not open to me? If so, it may be an impersonal good without being good for me. I will return to this possibility in the next chapter.

2 The personal value of perpetual survival

The argument from the absence of a beneficiary

To see the force of the case for the thesis we need first to dissociate it from some unsuccessful arguments for it. Perhaps the best known is the argument that if survival is good for the survivors, death must be bad for them.[5] But death cannot be bad for people before they die, since it has not happened yet. And it cannot be bad for them after they die for they are not there any more to suffer that bad. Since after one's death one does not suffer the loss of one's life its loss cannot be bad for one, and therefore survival cannot be good for one.

The argument is paradoxical in that it amounts to saying that the loss of one's life cannot be a loss for having lost one's life there is nothing one can lose. Surely, this is wrong

---

[5] Here as throughout I accept that if death (as against dying) is bad this is merely because of what it deprives the dying of. This view is sometimes called the deprivation view of the badness of death. But, as will appear later, I do not accept that survival is all that death can deny us. It also affects the meaning of our life before we die, for good or ill. It can deny us opportunities while alive.

for having lost one's life the loss, if it is one, has already occurred. It is wrong to say that having lost one's life one is no
longer there to suffer that loss, that is, the loss of one's life. The
absence of the subject of the loss after his or her death is neither here nor there. The question is whether had one not died,
had one lived longer, one's survival would have been good for
one. That can be the case in various ways. For example, it is
possible that had one lived longer one's life would have been
better and more successful overall. Or, it could be that one's
character would have improved, and one would have become
a better person. If so, staying alive would have been good for
one. The absence of a subject after death is neither here nor
there.

The value of mortality

A more serious objection is that mortality is vital to
our experience. Our experience of many things which are good
(and bad) is bound up with their temporality and finality,
bound up with the fact of scarcity, with the fact that choice
involves a forgoing: choose a career, a lover, a game of soccer. If
you could forever replay the game, change partners or careers
without loss, etc., then they would not have the meaning they
have. My point is not that they would have no meaning. Only
that we cannot get more of what is good in *our lives* by living
forever.

Similarly, every significant increase in longevity changes meanings. This is becoming clear in our own lifetime, as, in
the prosperous countries, longevity has increased by a significant amount over the last century. The meaning of retirement

and work has changed. Child-bearing periods and phases of life have changed, etc.

Does this matter? Possibly the values we can realise in our life are mostly bound up with our mortality. Nevertheless, were we immortal, positional goods would still be scarce: only one person can be my first lover, only one house my first house, and so on. Being John's lover before being Mary's has a different feel to it than had the relationships happened the other way round. Similarly being a shepherd who had been a lawyer is not the same in meaning as being a lawyer who had been a shepherd. The position of goods will invest them with specific meanings. They do today, and would do so, even if in a different way, were people to be immortal. Scarcity and the significance of choice will not disappear with mortality. The fact that increased longevity changes the meanings of available options, but does not eliminate meanings altogether, illustrates this point.

The arguments based on the positive value of mortality have, therefore, one crucial weakness. They establish that some, perhaps even many, of the valuable options realisable by human beings presuppose some qualities of our experience or of our capacity to have experiences, which in turn presuppose our mortality, or a longevity roughly as we have it. Radical changes in longevity will therefore make those options unavailable to people. It does not follow, and the arguments do not establish, that the very facts of scarcity that give choice and engagements their poignancy will disappear with radical increase of longevity.

Still, these arguments are instructive inasmuch as they correct one common mistake. Some people think that increased longevity will give them more opportunities to enjoy the valuable options they know of. This may happen if they enjoy a marginal increase in longevity. If that is what they desire, immortality will disappoint them. Immortality or a very significant extension of their life, whatever benefits it may bring, will not bring the benefits we know of today. Rather it will remove the valuable options we can have today, and will lead to others, unknown to us. Those who were looking for more or more and better of the same will be disappointed.[6]

It is time to enter three caveats regarding the scope of the preceding argument, caveats which apply to what follows as well. First, the argument assumes that longevity or immortality is achieved by all. I believe that situations in which one person only is immortal or enjoys longevity far in excess of that of everyone else differ only in degree. Perhaps other distributions (half and half, a third and two-thirds, etc.) are more interesting, but their consideration will not affect the basic argument above. Second, I am assuming general shared knowledge of the basic facts of people's longevity. Indeed, it can be claimed that the preceding argument is about the consequences of belief in immortality or long longevity, rather than about the consequences of these facts themselves. Third, I am ignoring questions about the possibility of suicide and the effect that possibility, were it to exist, would have on the meaning of options in our lives. While true, these observations do not undermine the force of the argument. For example, short of major efforts to perpetuate massive deceit, on a scale not hitherto

---

[6] This depends, of course, on how pervasive is the dependence of the goods available to people in their life on the rough current duration of people's life. I assume that it is very extensive indeed. But this is open to challenge.

achieved by humans, the facts of immortality would soon become common knowledge. Besides, the large-scale undesirable consequences of such ignorance and deceit should rule out any attempt to pursue them.

All that having been said, we have to recognise that the preceding considerations do not really bear on the intrinsic value of everlasting life. They are about the contents of such life, not about the life itself. Do they not mean that life is of value even if its contents change? Nothing in the points made above casts any light on this question. We can still maintain the thesis that life is of no intrinsic value, that the value resides not in life itself, but only in its content. Life is, we can maintain, merely a precondition of those contents.

Lucretius' argument

Another well-known, but ultimately unsuccessful, argument for the thesis derives from Lucretius. Lucretius argued that death cannot be bad for the dead, relying, among other reasons, on the asymmetry argument. If their death is bad for people, this cannot be so because of the badness of non-existence at a time one could have been alive (as the deprivation account seems to require). If death were bad in that way, argued Lucretius, this is because our non-existence is bad. However, if our post-mortem non-existence is bad, must we not concede that so is our non-existence before birth? If we are right to think that dying at a certain time is worse than dying later, then we should also believe that being born at a given time is worse than being born earlier. However, we do not regard the fact that we were born when we were rather than earlier as a bad for us. Therefore, nor should we regard dying when we die rather than later as bad for us.

The argument convinced a few to revise their views about pre-natal non-existence,[7] and many other writers sought to avoid its conclusion by denying the asymmetry between pre-natal and post-death non-existence.[8] I will suggest that both responses miss the point. They fail to notice that Lucretius' argument involves two distinct attitudes, one to length of life (preferences regarding longevity), and the other to the time at which this life will take place (preferences regarding location in time). Once the relationship between the two is properly understood the argument disappears, but we gain a better and more nuanced understanding of possible reasonable attitudes to death.

Some people think that they would be better off, or that their life would be better, if they lived longer than they are

[7] See, e.g., F. Feldman, 'Some Puzzles about the Evils of Death', *The Philosophical Review*, 100 (1991), 205, at 223.

[8] One influential argument in that direction was T. Nagel's, who argued (in 'Death' in *Mortal Questions*, Cambridge: Cambridge University Press, 1979) that, some minor changes in the time of birth apart, it is impossible for people to be born earlier than the time they were (since their identity is fixed by their DNA, which is determined at conception), whereas they could die much later than the time they die. Nagel was never confident that this asymmetry explains our different attitudes to pre-natal and post-mortem non-existence, and he somewhat modified his view in *The View From Nowhere* (Oxford: Oxford University Press, 1986). His impossibility of earlier birth claim was revived in a different form by F. Kaufman, whose argument depends not on bare identity, but on some notion of thick identity of the person one evolves into during one's life (see 'Pre-Vital and Post-Mortem Non-Existence', *American Philosophical Quarterly*, 36 (1999), 1, at 10ff.

going to live. The same people may also conceive a fancy to live at a different time from the time they actually live. They may even believe that they would have been better off in such a case, or that their life would have been better. They may think that they would have been better off had they lived at some past period which they regard as ideal, or particularly suitable for their temperament, for example. Or, they may wish to have been born at a later period when a cure would be available for some disability they suffer from, or when some talents they possess would win greater appreciation, as they think.

Clearly, beliefs of the second kind (desirability of temporal location) are distinct from and independent of beliefs of the first kind (desirability of longevity). One can have a belief about the desirability of enjoying a different location in time without believing in the value of greater longevity. Similarly, one can believe in the value of greater longevity without holding any view about the merit of different locations in time.

It is true that one's longevity affects one's location in time. One has to have lived at least to a hundred and thirty to have witnessed both the burning of Moscow and the siege of Leningrad. Furthermore, many people's views about the desirability of their own longevity are influenced by the consequences it will have for their location in time: some people want to have five more years in order to see their grandchildren, who they hope will be born by then; others want to die soon to avoid being alive at the death of their children, or to avoid witnessing some dreaded events. However much views about the desirability of different locations in time affect one's views about the desirability of one's longevity, the two are logically independent. One need not have any view about the relative merits of different locations in time to believe in the value to oneself of one's longevity.

People who regard death as an evil in itself (and not because of some contingent consequences it may have for them or for others) may be confused in a variety of ways. If there is a non-confused, true view which can be naturally expressed by saying that death in itself is an evil, it is likely to be the view that a longer life is, in and of itself, better than a shorter one. That is the view that longevity is intrinsically valuable, even if in some circumstances its benefits may be outweighed by the evil or unfortunate contents of one's life. However, if that is what people mean when they say that death is bad for one then there is no asymmetry between pre-natal and post-mortem existence implied by their view. They regret the fact that they will die at twenty or forty or eighty or whatever rather than have ten, or twenty, or thirty more years to live.

On this interpretation, Lucretius is wrong in thinking that people's preference for longevity is unwarranted because it manifests an unwarranted post-mortem/pre-natal asymmetry. It manifests no such asymmetry, for it involves no location preference, only a preference regarding longevity. Only a location preference, however, can manifest the asymmetry, and no such preference is necessarily involved in the preference for greater longevity.

Possibly this is a misreading of Lucretius' argument. It can be understood to claim that people have two common preferences. People (a) prefer greater longevity, and (b) prefer to have the extra years that greater longevity will bring after the time they would otherwise die rather than before the time at which they were in fact born. This second preference manifests the asymmetry. But, Lucretius' argument proceeds, since the first preference is in itself indifferent as to where the extra life be situated, that is, whether it be before birth or after death, it follows from it that people's second, location, preference is unwarranted. As the asymmetric location preference is (virtually) universal and reasonable it follows that the preference for longevity is unwarranted.

This argument, however, is clearly invalid. Its conclusion would follow only if further premises were added to it. For example, those who have the longevity preference may be embarrassed if they also believe that it entails the asymmetric location preference, or if they think that without the asymmetric location preference it would be irrational to have the longevity preference which they have. Or, the asymmetric location preference may be irrational in itself, but without it people would not have a preference for greater longevity. And there are other ways of supplying other assumptions about the relations between the two preferences which may embarrass those who hold both.

I am not aware of any true premises which have that effect. It is natural for any person expressing a preference for having a longer life to equate it with a preference for staying alive longer, that is, for not dying for some time to come. That is due simply to the fact that changing the past (by changing one's date of birth) is impossible, and so is any thought of placing the extra life one believes would be good for one at any temporal location other than contiguous with one's current life and proceeding into the future. The asymmetry that Lucretius detected is not in what is desirable (post-mortem rather than pre-natal life) but in what is believed to be a more feasible, or a less impossible way (continued life rather than backdated one) of achieving what is desirable (greater longevity). That object of desire itself displays no asymmetry, nor do people generally have an asymmetric location preference.[9] They only have a belief about the asymmetry between the power to change the past and the power to change the future.

Surely, I am missing something. Suppose that the Genie comes out of the bottle and, in reply to my wish, offers me ten extra years. Generously he leaves it to me to choose between changing my past so that I will die right now, but aged eighty rather than seventy, having lived ten more years, or changing the future so that I will still die at eighty but in ten years' time. Is it not clear that I will choose the second, and that that is the asymmetry Lucretius relies on?

Perhaps it is not all that clear which option people may choose. Some may have a special past-related wish. A devoted communist may wish he had been born ten years earlier so that he would have met Lenin. He may choose to have the extra ten years in the past. So may a person who has reason to think that not much good lies ahead of him in the future. On the other hand, some people are ruled by a desire to know the world in general and human history in particular. They will choose to extend their life into the future on the ground that while they can have second-hand knowledge of the past

---

[9] Except in the trivial sense that they want their longevity preference to be realised in the only way in which it can be, i.e., by extending their life into the future.

they will not know what lies in the future, unless they are alive then.[10] This contingent past/future asymmetry is not the kind Lucretius relies on. We can, however, neutralise factors like these by assuming that the Genie assures us that the quality of our life, relative to our wishes as they are now, or as we may believe they will change in the future, will be the same whichever option we choose. So neutralised it seems plausible to think that people will prefer to extend their life into the future, rather than into the past.[11]

[10] I am grateful to Ken Ehrenberg for drawing this possibility to my attention.

[11] Tom Nagel suggested a way of thinking about this possibility without invoking a magic power to change the past. Suppose the Genie tells you: 'it may be the case that you were in fact born 1 0 years before the time you think you were. I can tell you whether this is so, and even restore your memory of all that happened to you during those years (up to the normal level in which you remember your past life). Do you want me to do so?' We may not care all that much about whether he does or does not. If he offers a choice between revealing to us the truth about the past and a chance of adding ten years to our life in the future (telling us in advance that the odds are the same) we are much less likely to choose knowledge of the past.

It must be admitted that these counterfactual judgements cannot be too secure. This, I believe, is not a weakness in the use, or this use, of counterfactuals. Our uncertainty about them reflects our uncertainty about our attitudes to various aspects of our existence. For example, one factor, not neutralised even by the Nagel version, is a preference people may have for being as they are. A change of their past life, and even a restored memory of their past, threatens to bring with it a change to their life which may change their own understanding of what they are like. Some may like that. Others find it very off putting. This factor in itself may explain some of our location preferences independently of any longevity preference, and that explanation too undermines rather than reinforces Lucretius' argument.

I do not think, however, that this is the asymmetry Lucretius' argument requires. The asymmetry reflects a location preference. To bear on the value of life the argument must connect it to a longevity preference. This it fails to do. Let me explain the point step by step. Distinguish two kinds of location preferences, corresponding to the two kinds of time series, the relational series determined by 'before/after/at the same time' relations of events, and the indexical series, determined by the relations 'now/later than now (in the future)/before now (in the past)'. The location preferences I have mentioned so far are relational preferences, preferences to live at the time of certain other events, or before them, etc. The claim that I misinterpreted Lucretius' argument understands it to assume that we all share one indexical location preference, whereas we do not all have another. We all prefer to live as far as possible into the future, whereas we do not prefer to be older now, that is, to have been born further away in the past than we were.

Is Lucretius' argument in better order once we recognise that it involves a move from an indexical location preference to a longevity preference or vice versa? Clearly not. We can concede (1) that people not only believe in the impossibility of changing the past, but that they also have an indexical location preference that more life be ahead of them than will be the case, and (2) that that shows an asymmetry in their attitude, for they do not have the analogous indexical location preference to have more life before birth than is the case. To succeed, Lucretius' argument has to establish that it is unreasonable to hold that indexical location preference alongside the preference for longevity. It can be shown that the indexical location preference does not entail a preference for longevity.

The story of the Genie has done that. There is, however, no way to proceed from that conclusion to the assertion of the incompatibility of holding both of them, nor to the incompatibility of the reasons for the two preferences. One may wish for longevity out of belief in the value of life, and have the indexical location preference for a variety of independent other factors.

Examine the possible reasons for the indexical location preference. First, these reasons will be independent of the value of longevity. If greater longevity is good because a longer life is better than a shorter one it is evident that it implies nothing about location. Remember the options in the Genie example: does either of them speak of a better life? To do that it must be the case that, other things being equal, my life would be better if I die at eighty in 2010 rather than if I die at eighty in 2000. But that is an absurd conclusion. My longevity is the same both times, and other things are held equal. There is nothing in the facts of this hypothetical which can make my life between 1920 and 2000 better than my life between 1930 and 2010. Suppose that I am already dead, and we are now at 2050 retelling past exploits of long-lost Genies. I would not be deemed to have been better served by either alternative (if this is difficult to accept it is because of the difficulty of making sense of changing the past. We tend to think that this is merely cheating, like falsifying my birth certificate, without changing anything else. If so, then that option is clearly worse, but that is not what the Genie offers).

So, what reasons might there be for the asymmetric location preference? One reason was mentioned above, that is, changing the past will change what we are like now, change our experiences and character. Some may like that, others recoil from the very thought. Another reason is that we prefer not to be facing death right now,[12] or in the near future, and that is independent of any preference for longevity.

How can a preference not to face death in the near future be other than a preference to extend one's life into the future? Of course, the two coincide, which is why we normally have no reason to distinguish between them, but if we are allowed Genies we can have our Genie trading some time in our past for not dying now. Suppose the Genie offers the following deal to people who are now eighty and who know that they will die in the next couple of months: they can either die as expected, or the Genie will change the past, denying them ten years of their life, with the loss of all they experienced in them, and making them now only seventy. In exchange they will have five more years before they die. If, as I suspect, some people will take the option of dying younger, but not yet, it follows that some people value not dying soon even at a cost to their longevity. In any case, the example shows that the two preferences are distinct and that only the preference not to die soon, and not the preference for longevity, displays a bias towards the future.

As one would expect, not everyone wishes not to die soon. Some people cannot wait to die. This in itself may alert us to the fact that it is distinct from any belief in the desirability

---

[12] That preference is in some ways similar to Frances Kamm's speculation that death may be bad because it means that 'everything for oneself is all over' (*Morality, Mortality*, Oxford: Oxford University Press, 1993, vol. I, *Death and Whom to Save from It*, p. 19). It is not the 'all over' aspect that I am pointing to but the absence of meaning in the bit of life which is still with us. This does not presuppose that the desire that life will not be all over is cogent.

of longevity.[13] On reflection, the separateness of the desire not to die soon is hardly surprising. Given that it is impossible to satisfy it without satisfying the desire for longer life, we cannot expect that ordinarily people will focus on the differences between them and between the reasons for them. However, we know that awareness of the proximity of death does affect people's attitude to their remaining life. Reactions vary greatly, from sinking into despair to hyper-activity, from dropping all ephemeral concerns to finish a book, etc., to dropping all 'life-transcending' objects to concentrate on intensifying the pleasures of every moment one is alive. Whatever the reaction, and whatever rational reactions may be, it is evident that our activities have a future-oriented aspect to them. We do what we do now in light of many background beliefs (that the world will continue on its normal course, etc.) and among them are beliefs about our own future. When these are dispelled our sense of our own life, of our control over what we are doing, and why, our sense of the point of our current activities, is shaken. Special circumstances aside, this is not, and cannot be, a desirable situation. It is very unsettling and threatening. Small wonder that we do not welcome it. Our desire not to die soon is an aspect of our attitude to the life we have, not of our attitude to the life death deprives us of.

Not everyone who shares the asymmetric location preference will find the reason just given satisfactory. Many may feel that their reasons are very different, even when they are

---

[13] The desire is an all-things-considered desire. It is doubtful whether it makes sense to think of an other-things-being-equal desire with this content. Consideration of this point involves tracing the phenomenology of such desires in greater detail than would be warranted here.

not sure what they are. My sole point was to establish by one example the compatibility of the asymmetric location preference and of at least some reasons for it, with the preference for longevity, and of at least some reasons for it. It was not my purpose to account for all the reasons people think they have for it, many of which may be incoherent and confused. One need not examine them to reject Lucretius' argument against the value of continued life.

3 The personal value of extending life

The basic argument

Are there sound arguments supporting the thesis that life is not of intrinsic value to the person whose life it is? Is it good for every person to continue living? To evaluate the thesis it is helpful to contrast it with a mild alternative. So let us examine the question, not whether eternal life is of intrinsic value to its possessor, but whether it is (intrinsically) good for every person to remain alive for a while longer.

The case of people whose remaining prospect is continuous severe and incapacitating pain, or just a life of vegetating, is relevant here. In such cases remaining alive, even for only a short time, is not for the overall good of such people. Is it, however, plausible to claim that even so, it is good for them to continue living, though that good is outweighed by the pain and suffering? Personally, I find this thought incomprehensible. Can the incomprehension be expressed as an argument? Perhaps thus: if there is intrinsic value in continued living as such, then it must be possible to explain what is that good.

All explanations of the good of a life turn on the good of some aspects of that life, that is, on the value of the content of the life, of what is happening in it. There is, however, no good content awaiting a person terminally ill who is suffering great pain.[14] Therefore, there can be no value in it.

If this is a good argument, it proves the thesis. The problem is that it presupposes what it seeks to establish. It presupposes that the good of a life is in its content not in the life itself. Putting the point in this way may mislead. It does not assume that there is or can be life without content. It merely presupposes that if life itself is of value then it is of value (though not necessarily of overriding, or overall value), whatever its content. The argument consists in saying that since life's content can be good or bad, some people may have nothing but bad in the life remaining to them, and therefore their continued survival will have no value at all. Can it prevail against someone who denies the premise and claims that there is value in any life regardless of its content? I claimed that if life itself is of value there would be an explanation of its value. However, even that is denied by some.

Possibly, there is life which is separate from all content, at least if content presupposes experiential content. Perhaps what we call 'vegetative life' is contentless. I do not know whether there is no experiential content in the life of people in irreversible coma. However, assume such a condition, that is, a condition where the person is alive, but does not, and will

---

[14] This is the assumption of the example. Of course, sometimes people in the terminal stages of painful cancer continue to write books during brief periods of respite from pain, or provide support to friends, etc. The example is simplified to make the life all dark.

never, have any experiences. Is such a life in itself of value to that person? Some people may say yes it is, for it is wrong to terminate such a life. Plainly, however, this reply presupposes more than can be accepted at this stage of our argument. It assumes that only the value of the life can make its termination wrong. Besides, the reply also assumes that our belief, if we have it, that terminating the life of such people is wrong is more secure than our view about the value, or otherwise, of their continued existence.

The example of life with no further experiences, however, cannot dispose altogether of the claim that survival is intrinsically good. Those who believe that it is may simply say that they never meant to include life without experience. They merely meant life with experience, whatever those experiences are, even if they are all only bad. Is their view plausible?

It has to be admitted that it chimes better with common opinion which finds the thesis that personal survival is not of value to the survivor hard to accept. The proposed substitute, that life is a precondition for anything either good or bad happening to one, while obviously true, falls short of matching the common belief in the value of life. Since survival is not all that matters, it may conflict with other values. Survival and being free of pain, or having meaningful experiences, or opportunities for meaningful activities, may be incompatible. When they are it may be that on balance death rather than survival is best for the individual concerned. But this is consistent with survival in itself being valuable, being good for the survivor.

The case of a life of severe and paralysing pain was meant to deny this, to show that sometimes survival is of no value at all to the survivor, that in no respect, to no degree is it good for him to remain alive. In such circumstances there is no loss whatsoever to the person concerned in his loss of life.

If this is a good argument against the claim that life with experience is intrinsically valuable, regardless of the content of the experience, then it need not rely on cases where the only remaining experiences are of severe pain. The supposition that only experiences of negative value will fall to a person would do to show that his remaining alive is of no value at all. I think that some alternative scenarios will be found as persuasive as the case of severe pain. For example, if the only experiences the people concerned will have are of extreme humiliation, many will be inclined to concede that their life is without any intrinsic value. However, if we assume that their experiences are all negative, but not severe, that they are, for example, experiences of pain only but of mild pain, then the example loses some of its immediate appeal. There can be various explanations of this apparent inconsistency.[15] For example, people may find it difficult to imagine that we can know that those who suffer mild pain only will never have any positive experiences, whereas we are all familiar with cases, or stories, of severe terminal pain,

---

[15] Strictly speaking, this worry is beside the point. The point is to establish that it is the content of life which may (or may not) be of value, not life itself. Life is a precondition for having experiences, for acting, for having relationships, but it is they not life which can be of value, or can fail to have value. The case of severe and terminal pain is good enough (though inconclusive) a reason for that conclusion. Where it may fall short is in the next stage of the argument. Suppose it is admitted that only the contents of life bear intrinsic unconditional value. Does it follow that the contents have overall negative value if one's remaining experiences will all be negative, though not extreme? I consider this question indirectly below when discussing when it is reasonable to desire to live longer.

and can readily imagine how it can be that nothing good remains to someone in that condition. We therefore follow the instruction to imagine that no good will happen to the people who are in severe pain, but instinctively refuse it in the case of people with only mild pain. That is why we react differently to the two hypotheses.

Whatever the truth of this explanation it has to be admitted, as mentioned above, that the case depends on the assumption that the value of a life is to be found in its contents, an assumption which some will deny. I know of no knock-down argument against them. All I can do is try to develop, step by step, an alternative view which is more plausible.

Is survival a component of a personal good?

With that point in mind we should examine yet another possibility: even if survival in itself is not of value to the survivor, it is possible that it is a good, at least in the sense that it is a component of what is good for people. If a sunny day on the beach is good, good for me, does it not follow that being alive on that day is part of what is good, since surely what is good is being alive on the beach rather than being there dead? It is, however, easy to establish that the example must be understood as showing that life is not part of the good but a precondition of anything good happening. A component of the good may be something which is itself good, but also contributes to a greater good composed of several elements. In this way the heat of the sun, the smell of the sea, the bright colours, the tactile sensations of the sand on one's body, the proximity of people enjoying themselves, swimming, sunbathing, playing ball, combine to make a sunny day on the beach into the good it is, each being good in itself,[16] but endowing the total experience with value greater than that of the sum of its parts. The examples of life without any value show that life cannot be this kind of a component of what is valuable.

Can it be a component of the good which is not good itself in isolation but contributes to the goodness of what it is a part of, in the way that each line in a beautiful pen drawing need not be beautiful in itself in order to contribute to the beauty of the drawing as a whole? The difficulty with this supposition is that life is also a component of what is bad for a person in exactly the same way in which it is a component of what is good for people. To be a component of a good is more than to be a condition for the occurrence of the good. The alleged good component has to contribute to the good of the whole, as every successful aspect of a drawing can be shown to be part of what makes the drawing as a whole a success. The existence of the world is a precondition of savouring the taste of good wine. But it is not part of the good of drinking good wine. Likewise being alive is a precondition of anything being good or bad for me, but it does not contribute to the value of any good. It is of course possible for something which is neither good nor bad in itself to be a constituent good of something good and a constituent bad of something else which is bad. What shows that life is not in that way both a good and a bad is that its

[16] Strictly speaking, these properties make the experience good only in some circumstances, and are not essentially good-making. Here and elsewhere in the book I disregard such niceties, and express myself conversationally when this does not affect the argument.

contribution to goods and bads, to all goods and to all bads, is the same. To be a component good the contribution has to be distinctive to that good.

Those who are not convinced by this argument and think that something can be a component of the good even if it contributes to all goods and to all bads in exactly the same way will not be able to derive anything ethically significant about the value of life from their scepticism. Given that it contributes to goods and to bads in the same way it is, if a component of the good, a component of the bad as well. Therefore, there are probably no ethical truths which presuppose that life is a component of the good.

4 The relevance of the desire to survive

Finally, we turn to the fact that many people want to stay alive. Does that not show that survival is an intrinsic good? Not if their desire to survive is confused or misguided. Arguably, the case of vegetative survival shows that those who just want to carry on living, whatever life may hold for them, are indeed either confused or misguided. Most people, however, do not mean that when they say that they want to continue living. Often they mean that they have to carry on for there is no one else to look after their parents, or that their death will be a great loss to their intimate friends, etc. When they do not regard life and the avoidance of death as a necessary means for some valued end they normally mean that they want to spend time on the beach again, to have the company of their friends and family, to see their children succeed in life and have families of their own, to write another book, etc.

105

In reflective moments people will distinguish two ways in which they may have such goals. I want to spend a week in Paris next year. I mean by this that one of the things I would like to do next year, if I am alive, is to spend a week in Paris. Someone else, call her Josephine, may also say that she wants to spend a week in Paris next year, meaning by this something somewhat different. Josephine may mean that she wants to spend a week in Paris and to be alive in order to be able to do so. So far as I am concerned no desire or goal of mine remains unfulfilled if I die before I spend a week in Paris. Not so Josephine. If she dies before her Parisian sojourn materialises, one of her goals remains unfulfilled. Likewise, I have no reason to strive to stay alive just in order to visit Paris, whereas she, if the visit to Paris is no mere desire but one of her goals, has.[17]

Clearly, my desire to visit Paris does not show that I regard survival as such as a good. But Josephine's case is different. Given the nature of her aim to visit Paris, clearly her own survival has become one of her (subsidiary) goals. Does it show that she regards it as intrinsically good or as a component of an intrinsic good? How could she? It is for her no more of a component of her desired end (a visit to Paris) than it is for me. We both need to be alive to be in Paris. So if it is not a component of the good to me nor can it be to her.

The difference between us is not in what we regard as good or worthwhile in our goal, but in the background conditions for our endorsing that good as our goal. The difference

---

[17] I am assuming that while mere desires are not reasons for their authors, goals to do what is valuable are. See *Engaging Reason* (Oxford: Oxford University Press, 2000), chapter 3. See for a similar distinction B. Williams, *Problems of the Self* (Cambridge: Cambridge University Press, 1973), p. 85.

between us is analogous to the difference between John and Joanna, who also aim to spend a week in Paris next year. When we probe their intentions we discover that John wants to do so, assuming that he gets extra leave next year. Joanna, on the other hand, wants to go even if this will require resigning her job. If John does not get the extra leave, his aim to go to Paris which was conditional on getting it just lapses. Not so for Joanna. If she does not get the leave and does not resign her job to go to Paris, she fails to accomplish one of her goals. If John fails to get to Paris in exactly the same circumstances, there is no goal of his which he failed to accomplish. To conclude, while John and Joanna pursue slightly different goals, in that he has a conditional whereas she has an unconditional[18] goal of going to Paris, the good they are pursuing is, so far as we know, the same: the good of being in Paris. The same is true of me and Josephine, notwithstanding the fact that my goal is conditional on remaining alive in a way in which hers is not. In normal circumstances, having survival as an unconfused goal is due not to the view that survival is a good or a component of any good, but to the fact that it is a condition for the fulfilment of an unconditional (in the relevant respect) goal one has.

Can one have unconfused and sensible goals which are not conditional on survival? Surely yes. Many of our goals relate to goods whose value is independent of our continued existence. The value of my learning something new depends on my being around to be informed by this knowledge. But the value of completing the construction of a bridge I am working on, or of a novel I have started, does not depend on my

---

[18] Most goals are implicitly conditional on a variety of circumstances. I assume that the specified condition is the only one on which they differ.

continued existence. Does it show that having their completion as a goal unconditioned by survival is reasonable? Not yet. To show that we need to show also either that my contribution to the goal is of a kind which it makes sense, it is reasonable to make unconditional by survival. It is one thing to aim to look after one's minor children, and stay alive to do so, and quite another to stay alive in order to watch *Brookside*, or *Ally McBeal*. The good in the goal must be of a kind to make it sensible to live for its sake. There is probably not much more one can say in the abstract about the nature of such goals.

It may be thought that all goals which will suffer from my absence, or where the goal itself essentially requires my presence, are suitable goals for me to live for. For example, if the goal is to look after my children to maturity then (as we normally understand what is good for children) it is vital that I – their parent – will look after them, not merely that someone will, and therefore it is reasonable that my goal will not be conditional on my survival. My goal is to survive to look after my children, not merely to look after them so long as I survive. But where my service to the goal is entirely dispensable, that is, if the value the goal is meant to realise will be as probably and effectively realised should I die before it is accomplished, then it is not reasonable to make that goal unconditional, even though the value the goal will realise does not itself depend on my survival.

However, one's indispensability for a goal's success is neither sufficient nor necessary for the suitability of goals to be unconditioned by survival. It is not sufficient, for I may have trivial and unworthy goals to the success of which I am indispensable. It is not necessary, for it can be reasonable for people to have an unconditional goal for the success of which their survival is superfluous (people too old to contribute to the war effort may have aimed to be alive to see the Nazis defeated).

I am reluctant to endorse any general prescription regarding which goals it is reasonable to hold unconditionally. Reflection on the problem may, however, have far-reaching theoretical implications. For example, it seems that most people would not endorse a simple maximising conception of reasonable desire to remain alive. That is, we think that it is not unreasonable for people to desire to remain alive to be able to pursue some worthwhile goals, even if they know that on balance the remaining part of their life will have in it more bad than good. This seems easy to accept when the worthwhile goals are of considerable importance to others, or to impersonal causes, or when people take them to be central to what their own life is about. But I think that people often want to remain alive to enjoy pleasures, or accomplish goals of which this cannot be said. It is possible that people are irrational in such cases, or motivated by fear of dying, or of various forms of dying, fears which may be rational in themselves. These matters require careful and extended examination beyond what would be appropriate here.

So far I have ignored three of the most important responses which people may give to themselves or to others in response to the question 'what is the point of carrying on (living)?', the three which appear to be the most plausible candidates for justifying claims (made by people about themselves) that one just wants to remain alive. The first is the hope or the desire to end one's life in a certain way, to give one's life a certain shape, or just to give its end a certain shape and content. We sometimes admire, or respect or otherwise value people because their life ended in a certain way, or had a certain shape. Any such general features of a life, or of its last stage, which can make it an object of respect or admiration, etc., can also become goals one reasonably wishes to achieve in one's own life.

Second, the hope of finding goals, experiences, and attachments that will make life meaningful again, the openness to such goals, or indeed the search for them. This can be a mere hope, or it can be a second-order goal, the goal of finding goals which will give meaning to one's life. It is, however, a very special goal: and notwithstanding its importance to the person whose goal it is, its satisfaction does not in itself contribute to the success of one's life. It may equally contribute to its failure. Typically, the life of a person with no goals and attachments is, and feels, meaningless. Typically, such people drift into despair, or cynicism, their dominant feeling being of the futility of everything. A hope of finding valuable goals and attachments, and the goal of finding them, stave off despair, keeping it at bay. The realisation of that hope, the satisfaction of the goal, is the finding of purpose and meaning in one's life. It is the finding of goals to be pursued, of attachments to be cultivated. It is, in other words, the opening up of the possibilities of success, but also of failure. It banishes the despair of emptiness, but sometimes replaces it with the cutting pain of failure and bitter disappointment.

Is it reasonable to stay alive in the hope of finding meaning, that is, goals and attachments? When that hope is reasonable, it is.

The third reason is one's pleasure in simply being alive. Consideration of the attitude expressed by saying: 'I do not need any reason to remain alive. I just enjoy living in itself' brings us to the insightful discussion by Nagel of what is bad about death.[19]

5 Nagel on the good of life

The bulk of his essay is concerned to establish four points which we should accept: first, that things can be bad for us even though they do not involve unpleasant experiences. (The collapse of a bridge one designed may show one to have been a bad architect, diminishing the success of one's life and therefore one's well-being even though one never finds out about it.) Second, the badness of death, if any, is merely in what it deprives us of, that is, in the fact that life is good for those who are alive and its loss is bad for them. Third, that the deprivation is a fact about one's life, or oneself, a fact, rather than an event that has to be located in time, and cannot be ascribed to the subject since it does not occur until the subject does not exist. Fourth, that the asymmetry between death and pre-natal non-existence is paralleled by the fact that dying when one does is accidental, whereas it is impossible to be born much before one is, for then a different person would have been born.

These points seem to me valid, as is Nagel's own doubt[20] whether his refutation of Lucretius' argument is correct. However, none of this affects the arguments above. From our point of view the crux of the matter is in the un-argued-for, though plausible-sounding assertions at the beginning of the essay, namely the contention that some of what is of value in life is so inseparable from life itself that life itself is of value.

[19] 'Death' in *Mortal Questions*, pp. 1–10.
[20] Expressed in the long note in *ibid.*, on p. 8.

He says: 'some of them [i.e., the goods in life], like perception, desire, activity, and thought, are so general as to be constitutive of human life. They are widely regarded as formidable benefits in themselves, despite the fact that they are conditions of misery as well as of happiness ... that is what is meant, I think, by the allegation that it is good simply to be alive, even if one is undergoing terrible experiences' (p. 2). Experience itself, Nagel concludes, is good, and makes life itself good, whatever its content (even if overall its good may be outweighed by the bad experiences one suffers).

When writing about activity, perception, and thought being part of life rather than contents which it may or may not have, does Nagel refer to the activities: perceiving, thinking, acting, or to the capacities for them, that is, the ability to think, act, and perceive? I am not sure what is Nagel's view. Clearly, he does not mean episodes of thinking, perceiving, or acting. These may be good or bad. It is not plausible to claim that there is always something good in them. Even if activity, thought, and perception are inseparable from life, no action, no episode of thought or perception is inseparable from it.

Nor is it plausible to claim that the disjunction of all our actions, thoughts, or perceptions is intrinsically valuable, nor even that the disjunction of all the thoughts, perceptions, and actions open to us is so valuable. The value of the disjunction is a function of the value of the disjuncts, and not independent of it. It is, in other words, a feature of the contents of our life as it is or may be, not of life independently of its contents.

Nagel seems to have a different idea in mind. He regards the goods he lists as what is left once one substracts both good and bad experiences from one's life (p. 2). But he also calls what is left 'experience itself' (*ibid.*). He may have in mind some experiential quality inseparable from being alive, or from being alive and able to think, perceive, and act, or inseparable from being awake with these capacities intact. If there is such an experience which is of intrinsic value it is inseparable only for the waking life of people whose capacities to act, think, and perceive have not been too radically impaired. It therefore cannot be regarded as inseparable from life itself, for sleeping people are also alive. It must be regarded as a relatively pervasive part of the content of our life. This point may be accommodated if we modify the thesis to claim that the waking life of those with a modicum of ability to think, perceive, and act is intrinsically valuable, for inseparable from it is an experience sometimes called 'the feeling of being alive' which is intrinsically valuable.

I will return to this suggestion below. First, let me pursue another thought, probably not Nagel's but suggested by his essay, namely that the abilities which are inseparable from being alive are intrinsically valuable, and in being so make life a good, and the longer the life the greater the good.

The abilities to act, think, and perceive can be taken as inseparable from life so long as the life whose continuation we are considering is restricted to life in which these capacities are present. Earlier we excluded life without experiences from consideration. The exclusion of life without the capacity for thought and action, and without perceptual ability, can be seen as a further specification of the kind of life in the longevity of which we are interested. Obviously, at least in part this specification is motivated by an understanding of what is of value in life (when that notion is more broadly understood). However, there is nothing amiss in proceeding in this way.

Does possession of these capacities have value which endows survival with intrinsic value to the survivor? The first doubt concerns the value of the abilities. There is no doubt that they have value, for without them it is impossible for people to have a life of activity and involvement with the world around them. Most, if not all, the valuable contents of our lives derive from our activities, and from our engagement with the world. That the abilities can be misused is no reason to doubt their value. Only if they can only be misused do they lose their enabling value, their value as preconditions of, and instruments for, whatever is of value in human life. That enabling value may not however be an intrinsic value. In spite of the many differences, it can be compared to the value of a tool. Having a car enables me to travel places. But its value is instrumental not intrinsic; it is valuable to me because I can use it for certain purposes. The value of a tool is that while I have it I am able to pursue certain goals, should they present themselves, and should I choose to pursue them. Ultimately the value is in the goals which will or may be pursued, not in the tool.

The value of abilities, it seems to me, should be understood in a similar way. They have enabling value. It is not exhausted by the value of the use made of them. They have an option value, a value in the ability to seize opportunities when they arise. But that too is a value on the way to intrinsic value, not an intrinsic value in itself.

This point may be lost sight of if we confuse the value of abilities with the value of choice. Most of the time when stating 'I was able to choose between . . .' one does not assert possession of any ability, but the presence of an opportunity to choose. Of course, paralysis and lack of certain mental abilities may deprive one literally of an ability to choose. But fortunately they are rare, and the need to assert them even rarer, so that the expression 'I am (or was) able to choose' and its cognates has acquired as its primary use reference to the opportunity of a relatively unhindered choice. In general, opportunities are, like abilities, enabling conditions. But on occasion things are different with the ability and opportunity to choose. While generally the value of an action is independent of the opportunities and abilities which made it possible, sometimes it is essential to its value that it was an expression of a free choice. In such cases, the presence of an ability and an opportunity to choose freely are an integral part of what is valuable about the action which made use of them. No lesson can be drawn from that regarding the value of abilities in general.

Abilities and opportunities are valuable, but their value depends on the prospect that they will be used wisely and successfully. Their value is conditional, and derivative. The claim that life itself is intrinsically valuable is interesting only if it is a claim that life has an unconditional and non-derivative value.[21]

---

[21] Abilities and opportunities play a prominent role in furnishing the grounds for hope that life will turn for the better in the future, and for the second-order goal to find worthwhile unconditional goals, which as we saw above can form a reasonable basis for a desire to remain alive. This is consistent with the enabling value of abilities and opportunities.

But am I not missing something crucial here? Ulrike Heuer has put it to me that only if I value myself as the author of my life does it make sense for me to pursue the possibility of finding something worthwhile in the future. Whatever truth there is here is about the value of people, not of their remaining alive. I will discuss the value of people in the next chapter.

We should return, then, to the way of understanding Nagel's claim which seems most promising, namely that certain valuable experiences are so pervasive as to be indistinguishable from life itself. As we saw, this claim is credible only if by life we mean a life of some experiential quality. The thesis is that an experienced life, in which the experience includes the experience of perception, of thought and of action has some good in it, regardless of what one experiences, regardless of the value of the content of one's experiences. Perhaps the way to make the point is that experiencing is good in itself, and experiencing is an aspect of all experience. Therefore, all experience, whatever its content, has a valuable aspect, has something which is intrinsically and unconditionally good about it.

How credible is this view? I will raise three doubts. (1) Does all experience possess this good aspect? (2) Is it of the right kind to make one's life better the longer it is? (3) Is it something it is reasonable to want to stay alive for? To my mind only the third has an affirmative answer.

It is significant that Nagel does not mention sensations among the fundamental aspects of experience which are inherently valuable. The reason is that some sensations, pain sensations and others, are intrinsically bad. The pleasure of just being alive is, however, saturated with valued sensations: the skin and one's muscles feel good, and one is full of the pleasure of living, even while just walking the street looking at familiar everyday sights. These feelings are real enough and valuable enough, but they are not pervasive enough to be inseparable from life and make life itself good. On the contrary, we are familiar with the complaint of people who used to wake up with a spring in their heel, and whose existence was suffused with a sense of well-being, and who have lost it, and now feel depressed, and morose, and achy, etc.

Is there anything in thought, imagination, and perception to make them different from sensations and feelings, and to show that they always possess a good aspect? I do not think so. Perception can become a source of pain and horror, as can thought and the imagination. It may happen, for example, that from the moment one wakes up, one may be afflicted with racing thoughts of torture, and persecution, which make any rational thought impossible, and one's eyes may be opened to a view of the world in extreme and violent colours, etc. I fear that the factors which make experience valuable are present only contingently and do not warrant the conclusion that life itself is a good.

This objection is sufficient in itself to refute Nagel's contention that life itself is intrinsically valuable. Even when we limit ourselves to conscious life, with the experiences or capacities of thought, imagination, action, etc., it turns out that it is not always and inescapably of any value to the people whose life is in question. It all depends on its content. For the sake of argument, however, let us dispense with this objection, and assume that all experience contains an intrinsically valuable aspect. Does it follow, as Nagel claims, that its deprivation through death is a loss?

It is natural to think that the loss is in the value of one's life. That is, it is natural to think that if remaining alive is of intrinsic and unconditional value to the person whose life it is this is because that person's life will be better if he or she remains alive longer, rather than dies now. It is tempting to understand the claim to be that since life is good (in and of itself), the more of it one has the better off one is (other things being equal). One is better off because (other things being equal) one's life is better if one lives longer, one would then have a better life (other things being equal).

We can agree that, other things being equal, a person who died at forty, having been fifteen years, not necessarily the last fifteen years, in a coma, would have been better off, and would have had a better life, had he not been in a coma at all. Does it follow from that that, other things being equal, a person who died at twenty-five would have been better off had he died at forty? One of Nagel's examples is meant in part[22] as an affirmative answer. He imagines a person who suffered a severe brain injury reducing him to the mental life of a baby, whose 'happiness consists in a full stomach and a dry diaper' (p. 6). We can agree that, other things being equal, that person suffered a misfortune, that his life is much worse than it would have been but for the injury. Does it follow, as intimated by Nagel, that had he died of his injury, his misfortune would have been in some ways similar, only greater, for he would have been deprived of the good that even his reduced life was?

Nagel appears to argue that if life is a good then its continuation is of value, for by living longer one has more of life, that is, more of the good that life is. More good is

---

[22] Though its main purpose is to support some of the four points listed above.

better than less. Something like this argument underlies the conclusion that it is better to have the goods of life throughout one's life, rather than to be in a coma for part of one's life. It is not that being in a coma is intrinsically bad for one, but rather that but for it one would have had more good, more which is of value in one's life. Does the argument apply to judgements of the value of different durations of life as Nagel assumes? This is not obvious. The answer may be yes and no. It may be, for example, that on the one hand, if every moment in life is a good then more of it is more of a good. On the other hand, however, it may be the case that having more of it, more of life, is not better for the people whose life it is. This may be so, for example, if it does not make their life better, it does not lead to them having a better life.

To illustrate the possibility suppose that *Roberto's* is one of the good restaurants in town. I have eaten there before, and every time it was time well spent, well-prepared, tasty food, in pleasant surroundings. If I go there again today it will be the same. I will have more of that good. But it will not necessarily make me or my life better if I do so. True, the pleasure of good food is important in life, but I have had plenty of it, and plenty of *Roberto's*. My life will not improve by having more of the same, good as it is. In *Roberto's* case the question whether I should dine at *Roberto's* tonight does not depend on whether doing so will make my life better. It depends on whether, given that I have a reason to dine at *Roberto's*, because the food and the ambience are pleasant, I have a better reason, or at least a reason which is no worse, to do something else instead. Options need not contribute to the value of our life to be the options we should pursue.[23] Pursuing them may even detract from the value of our life (as is sometimes the case when our only choice is between evils). We should follow options which are best supported by reason whatever their impact on our life.

Nagel's argument, however, purports to show that more of life is better than less of it, whatever its content. The fact that every moment of it is a good does not show that. At least it does not show that without further premises. In general, many of the goods of our life do not make our life better. They are too insignificant and unconnected with what we care about in our life to do that. Having another ice cream now may be a good thing to do, and it may not conflict with anything I have better reason to do, but whether or not I have the ice cream will not, special circumstances apart, affect the quality of my life. Being alive a bit longer, enjoying the goods of perception, thought, and action may well likewise not affect the quality of my life as a whole. Whether or not it does depends on the contents of my perception, thought, or action.

If my life is not better for being longer then my personal survival is not an intrinsic and unconditional good for me. I argued for this conclusion on the assumption that we are not merely looking for something good which will happen to us if we remain alive, but that having the extra good will be good for us, and in particular that it will be good for us in making our life better. I argued that just having more good things or experiences in our life will not necessarily make our life

---

[23] Nor, of course, do we, nor should we, pursue them to maximise good in our life. I do not go to *Roberto's* tonight in order to have more of this or any other good in my life, but simply because given my situation that is a good thing to do.

better, and therefore it will not necessarily be good for us. It is true, of course, that it will mean that something worthwhile happened to us, or that we did something worthwhile, or had some worthwhile experience. That shows that there is good in our life, regardless of whether it makes our life better. What does that establish? It establishes that we do not have to commit suicide, nor to prefer to be dead than alive. I may prefer to remain alive in order, let us assume, to enjoy these goods. After all, while dying may not be bad for me it is not better than living either. If my life has the pervasive goods which sensation, perception, imagination, thought, and action, can bring, some of which Nagel has in mind, it would be natural for me to want it to continue, even though it is not, other things being equal, irrational of me to prefer it to end.

6 Fear of death, and the view from within

It is not only the love of life which keeps us going. So does the fear of death. Conceptually distinct, they are closely interwoven throughout most of our lives. The phenomenology of our attitudes may seem at odds with the Epicurean view I have defended. Certainly its expression in the sentence 'death is nothing to us' is provocative precisely because it is so much at odds with our sentiments, especially with our fear of death. The provocation was, no doubt, intended. Its rhetorical force may or may not be welcome, but should not obscure the underlying truth. If truth it is. The doubt is that it is at odds with our visceral emotions, our fear of death, our clinging to life, our zest for life.

Part of the difficulty in assessing these doubts is the obscurity of the emotions they appeal to. Do we fear death because we love our lives and what we fear is losing what we love, or do we fear death independently of how we feel about our life? There is some evidence that the second is often the case, that is, that even people who are deeply unhappy about their life fear death. But normally these feelings and emotions are intertwined and indistinct. Do we fear death or do we fear dying? Probably both, but again the feelings are most commonly too indistinct for a neat analysis. Do we fear death because of the loss of life we would have if we do not die, or do we fear death because it unsettles our attitudes to the life remaining to us before we die? I suggested earlier that the second is a factor, but clearly not the only one.

In these and other ways our fear of death is not a perspicacious emotion, or feeling. People's descriptions of their attitudes to their own death, or to that of people close to them, reveal a range of attitudes and emotions, some very powerful. Often they are rationally indefensible, or even nonsensical, if taken literally, even though they are illuminating and evocative when taken metaphorically or as an *as if* description of what they feel. It seems to me that we should recognise that something like fear of death is a native emotion with human beings, perhaps an emotion which makes life possible. At any rate, it makes the prospect of continued life more unquestioned than it would otherwise be. Its expression in words and images is probably highly culturally dependent and should be subject to rational assessment; it is often based on superstitions and false beliefs.

The indistinct character of the underlying fear suggests that it lies in between moods and emotions, being in some ways more like anxiety, vague and unfocused, with the potential to overpower the subject when growing into an anxiety attack. Moods are not subject to the same rational assessment that governs emotions. Not being so-called 'propositional attitudes' they do not have objects, nor are they essentially based on beliefs and evaluations ('this creature is dangerous', etc.) as are emotions. They can be, of course, welcome or unwelcome, desirable or otherwise. If the views expressed here tend to undermine some of the feelings/moods towards death which govern some of our lives, they may be none the worse for that. This is, after all, why Epicurus chose to be provocative.

4

Respecting people

1 Introduction

One thing is clear. If people's continued life is not intrinsically and unconditionally good for them then the value of continued life to the people whose life it is cannot underpin the requirement to respect the life of others. The fact that life is a precondition of the value which the content of that life may have is neither here nor there. The requirement to respect the life of others is not subject to the variations which affect the value of the contents of the life of people. Our duty to respect people's life does not vary in scope or strength with variations in the value of the content of the life of those people. Possibly, it is somewhat sensitive to the value of those people's lives. We may not owe the same respect to the life of murderers as to the life of others. Our duty to respect the life of others, however, does not vary in tune with every fluctuation in the value of the contents of the life of those others.

This conclusion is not as worrying as it may appear, if only because it is inevitable for independent reasons anyway. For example, the value of survival to the survivors could at most contribute to an explanation of why we should respect their *life*. However, when thinking of duties of respect for people the objects of respect are *people*, not their life. I am not suggesting that respecting people has nothing to do with respecting their life. Respect for people may be a reason to respect their life, and I will

124

return to this. The latter is, however, only one aspect of respect for people. It involves, for example, certain ways of thinking of them, and ways of talking about them and to them, which have no connection with the prospect of their survival. They are aspects of respecting people, not of respecting their lives.

Respect for people is, and is generally acknowledged to be, a central moral duty. The argument below will help explain that. There is no denying that respect for this or that, including respect for people, is often morally required. It is less clear whether respect for people does occupy a pivotal role in ethics or in practical thought more generally. One view holds respect for people to lie at the foundations of all moral duties. One version of such a view combines it with a conception of morality as based on reciprocity. Moral persons owe respect to each other, and the rest of morality follows.[1] One has to be a moral agent, a person bound by the moral law, to be a moral patient, someone towards whom moral agents have moral obligations. Constructive or contractualist conceptions of morality tend to be variants of reciprocity-based conceptions of morality.[2] An ethic of reciprocity appears, however, unduly restrictive, and insensitive, to those who believe that we have duties to future generations (who cannot have reciprocal duties towards us), to members of other animal species, and towards the environment, or aspects of it. There are other objections to reciprocity and constructivist conceptions of ethics, but

---

[1] This is the ethics of respecting persons discussed and ably criticised by W. K. Frankena in 'The Ethics of Respect for Persons', *Philosophical Topics*, 14 (1986), 149.

[2] Though they need not all place the duty of respecting people centre stage.

I will not discuss them here. I will concentrate on other ways of understanding the place of respect for people in morality.

An easy way of equating the scope of the duty of respect with the scope of morality is to hold that we respect others when we behave towards them as we morally ought to behave, and that we show lack of respect when we fail to do so, in culpable circumstances. On this view there is no specific source for duties or reasons to respect others. Rather, moral reasons arise out of whatever valid moral concerns can generate reasons, and once we know what morality requires on those independent grounds we can know what we ought to do to respect people (or the environment, or whatever), namely, we ought to conform to the valid moral requirements.[3] This by-product view of respect, towards which I tended to lean once upon a time,[4] denies that there is something distinctive about duties of respect, setting them aside from other duties, including other moral

---

[3] A version of this view is expressed by H. Frankfurt when he writes: 'Treating a person with respect means, in the sense that is pertinent here, dealing with him exclusively on the basis of those aspects of his particular character or circumstances that are actually relevant to the issue at hand. Respect, therefore, entails impartiality and the avoidance of arbitrariness.' 'Those who wish to treat people with respect aim at outcomes that are matched specifically to the particularities of the individual' (see his 'Equality and Respect' in *Necessity, Volition and Love* (New York: Cambridge University Press, 1999), p. 150). His view is more complex than this. I discussed and criticised it in 'On Frankfurt's Explanation of Respect for People', in S. Bass and L. Overton (eds.), *Contours of Agency: Essays in Honour of Harry Frankfurt* (Cambridge, Mass.: MIT, forthcoming).

[4] In *The Morality of Freedom* (Oxford: Oxford University Press, 1986), p. 157, I equated respecting people with treating them in accordance with sound moral principles.

duties. Moreover, it denies that there are special reasons to re-spect people, irrespective of other reasons for treating them this way or that. It denies that concern for respecting people is an independent moral concern. That makes it less plausible. I am inclined to think that we should accept it only if a more substantive understanding of reasons for respect proves elusive.

Some see the special role of a doctrine of respect for people as determining status.[5] It determines not how to treat people morally, but that people are of moral concern. They enjoy a moral status, and therefore one should look for moral reasons, moral duties or prohibitions regarding their proper treatment. Plants, according to some, differ from people in that regard. There is no doctrine of respect for plants, and that means that they do not enjoy moral standing. They do not count, as people say. Therefore, we need not seek for moral prohibitions, or duties, regarding the ways they must or must not be treated.

Such doctrines of status are not, however, easy to un-derstand. David Copperfield, when a child, is forbidden to play with Peggotty, because one should not play with servants. We can imagine that his case, as understood by his stepfather, is governed by two kinds of considerations – call them con-siderations of intrinsic merit and of status. Considerations of intrinsic merit determine that an appropriate playmate is one who is willing to play in a friendly, co-operative spirit, abide by the rules, be fun, etc. In all these ways Peggotty is a very suit-able playmate. However, considerations of status determine

---

[5] In the main this and the next three paragraphs are incorporated from 'On Frankfurt's Explanation of Respect for People'.

that one should not associate with members of a social class lower than one's own, and therefore, even though intrinsically she is a good playmate, one may not play with her.

This is the way that some people understand doctrines of moral standing, and they reject them for the same reasons which make us suspicious of the social-status rule which helped to ruin part of Copperfield's childhood, and was so unfair to Peggotty. According to them: people can suffer from pain, and hunger, and other afflictions, and so can other mammals. Intrinsic considerations show that it is wrong to cause pain and other afflictions to mammals, human or otherwise. The only possible effect of introducing a separate doctrine of status is to deny the application of reasons where they do in fact apply. Whereas we must respect people, there is no similar doctrine of respect regarding other mammals, and therefore, we must not cause pain to people, but there is no reason not to cause pain to other mammals, since they do not count. But if the reason for not causing pain applies to all animals, how could a doctrine of status absolve us from following it? If, as some may think, there is no reason to refrain from causing pain to animals of other species, would not that have to be a result of the content of the reason to refrain from causing pain (i.e., it would be a reason which does not apply to other animal species), and not a result of a doctrine of status whose effect is to exempt us from following reasons where they apply?

The question is: once a reason to treat someone in some way is established, what room is there for a doctrine of respect to determine who counts? Is it not plain that so far as that reason goes all those to whom it applies count and that is the end of the matter? And the same goes for any other reason. So if there is reason not to hurt, that reason applies to those who can be hurt; a duty not to kill would apply to all those who can be killed, etc. Of course, if the duty not to kill is explained by reasons which do not apply to all living creatures, then it would not apply to all. If we should not kill because we should not abbreviate people's expectation of life, or because we should not prevent people from conceiving and engaging in worthwhile enterprises, then we should not kill any animal whose expectations of life would thereby be curtailed, or whose ability to conceive and engage in worthwhile activities would be interrupted. Not all animals, indeed not all human animals, will meet this condition, and therefore not all of them are protected by the injunction against killing. The details of the example do not matter. What matters is that there is no room, or so the argument goes, for a doctrine of status to determine the scope of application of reasons or duties. The grounds of those reasons or duties determine their scope.

These doubts do not refute a status-conferring understanding of a doctrine of moral respect. In particular it is possible that many (moral) reasons apply to our attitudes and actions towards people and others who meet certain conditions. Those conditions can perhaps be seen as a precondition of enjoying a standing in ethical matters, and their specification and the explanation of their implications can be the doctrine of respect. In a way this is the route I will be following in the reflections below, though if that route is the right one there is nothing gained from, and there is some danger of being misled by, thinking about respect as a status-conferring doctrine.

An obvious alternative to the approaches mentioned so far is one establishing a distinctive duty to respect others (whoever they may be) such that all other moral duties or requirements are derived from it, perhaps even are instances of it. This seems to me unlikely.[6] If the explanation of respect below is along the right lines, the impossibility of deriving the whole of morality from a doctrine of respect will become apparent.[7]

In the arguments that follow I will not assume that the common understanding of our duties to respect others (is there such?) is correct, and that the task is merely to understand why the duties it assumes are valid. It is possible that our common understanding of such duties is misguided, and should be corrected. Advances in biotechnology have in any case put pressure on our views about our basic duties towards other people, and led many to reconsider their opinions. I suspect that the conclusions arrived at here are at odds with many common beliefs. However, it is not my aim to establish the shape and degree of this discrepancy. I am merely interested in the reasons for our duties towards other people which are established by a doctrine of respect.

2 Kantian origins

As will emerge below, my understanding of respect for people is similar to Kant's. It is ironic, however, that while

---

[6] Partly for reasons explained by Frankena, 'The Ethics of Respect for Persons'.

[7] In *Engaging Reason* (Oxford: Oxford University Press, 2000), chapters 11 and 12, I argued that there is no significant division between moral and other reasons. The present chapter continues that argument indirectly. If it is right, it shows that we cannot identify morality with the requirements, duties, and other concerns which follow from a doctrine of respect.

the attraction of *personal respect* (as I will call the kind of respect for people we aim to explore) is due in no small part to the impact of Kant's moral philosophy, Kant's own writings on *respect* contribute little to twentieth-century thinking about the subject. Current discussions of respect for people have moved away from Kant's understanding of respect. My critique of some of them is partly a return to a more Kantian position.[8]

One difficulty in understanding Kant is due to the fact that his view about respect is bound up with his dualistic understanding of people as having a phenomenal and a noumenal aspect. In the following comments I will disregard the dualistic aspect of Kant's thought and will look for an account of respect that does not depend on it. This means, of course, that I will not be trying to give an authentic interpretation of Kant's own view, but rather of some aspects of it.

Considering practical reason Kant says:

> Respect for the moral law is therefore the sole and also the undoubted moral incentive, and this feeling is also directed to no object except on this basis. First, the moral law determines the will objectively and immediately in the judgement of reason; but freedom, the causality of which is determined only through the law, consists just in this: that it restricts all inclinations, and consequently the esteem of the person himself, to the condition of compliance with its pure law. This restriction now has an effect on feeling and produces the feeling of displeasure which can be cognised a priori from the moral law ... But the same law is yet objectively – that is, in the

[8] On personal respect. I do not mean to imply that what follows contributes in any way to a Kantian understanding of morality generally.

131

representation of pure reason – an immediate determining
ground of the will, so that this humiliation takes place only
relatively to the purity of the law; accordingly, the lowering
of pretensions to moral self-esteem – that is, humiliation
on the sensible side – is an elevation of the moral – that is,
practical – esteem for the law itself on the intellectual side;
in a word, it is respect for the law, and so also a feeling that
is positive in its intellectual cause.[9]

Two interrelated questions are raised by this passage. On its
face it claims that the will is determined by the moral law, a
determination which is an expression of our freedom as well
as of our rationality. 'The moral law determines the will ob-
jectively and immediately in the judgement of reason.' If so,
however, what is the role of respect for the moral law? It is said
to be 'the sole ... moral incentive'. This may mean that it is
nothing but recognition of what is required of us by the moral
law, recognition of the moral law. The tail end of the quotation
suggests, however, that 'respect' cannot be identified with pure
rational determination of the will. Here Kant associates it with
a *feeling* of 'esteem for the law itself', though 'respect' is not
identified with such a feeling. Rather the esteem for the moral
law 'in a word ... respect for the law' is 'also a feeling that is
positive in its intellectual cause'.

An additional puzzle is the fact that Kant treats practical reason differently from theoretical reason. There is no analogue to respect in his treatment of theoretical reason. But if

[9] *Critique of Practical Reason*, ed. M. Gregor (Cambridge: Cambridge
University Press, 1997), pp. 67–8 (5: 78–5: 79).

reason can determine the will to believe one thing or another, with no special feeling of respect being invoked, why can it not determine the will to will one thing or another without such feeling? An obvious answer, suggested in the quotation, is that only practical reason encounters the resistance of our inclinations and self-love. This seems to me to be mistaken, as self-love, wishful thinking, vanity, etc., can and often do distort our judgements. The humbling of inclination and self-love does not appear to justify the disanalogy between Kant's treatment of practical and theoretical reason.[10]

Be that as it may, the relevance of self-love and inclinations to respect for the moral law is not easy to comprehend. What conquers them and makes us follow the moral law is

[10] Kant also relies on his doctrine of freedom to explain the difference between practical and theoretical reason. I do not believe that his discussion of freedom helps with the problem I pose here, but I will not stop to argue the case here. For my general view of the relation between freedom and practical reason see chapter 1 of *Engaging Reason*. It is not my assumption that the shape and structure of failures to follow reason in theoretical and practical matters are identical. For the purposes of the present argument all that is required is that analogous irrationalities can exist in both cases. In particular, it is possible to believe that all things considered one should perform an action without performing it, or even intending to perform it. Perhaps there is no exact analogue of this in the relation between believing that there is overriding reason to believe that so and so and believing that so and so. Though, possibly, one can feel that while all the evidence is that so and so one cannot quite bring oneself to believe that that is so. If so, then the analogy is far reaching. But even if it is only partial, the case I am making stands. The existence or non-existence of a special motivation (respect for the moral law) cannot be needed to explain this particular form of irrationality any more than it is needed to explain others.

the moral law itself,[11] or if you like, our recognition, as self-legislators and members of the kingdom of ends, of our moral duty. If so, then respect is relegated to being a by-product, a feeling which arises in us as our will is determined by the moral law.

Whichever way we resolve the interpretive doubts it appears that Kantian respect has little to do with contemporary thinking about respecting people. The moral law, rather than people, is the object of respect. And there are no duties or requirements to respect anyone or anything. Rather, (a feeling of) respect arises in us as the moral law determines our will. Contemporary discussions of respect for persons strive to articulate and defend a particular moral principle or doctrine, that is, the one saying, in brief, that we must respect people. That principle has little to do with Kant's doctrine of respect, which, to repeat, does not add to the content of morality, but says that whenever we perform an action because we rationally believe that it is our moral duty to do so we act out of respect for the moral law. It is true that Kant is happy to extend respect to objects other than the moral law itself, but when used in this way respect derives from respect for the moral law.

---

[11] While at the beginning of the quotation above Kant regards respect as the moral incentive, elsewhere he says: 'What I recognise immediately as law for me, I recognise with reverence [= respect] which means merely consciousness of the subordination of my will to a law without the mediation of external influences on my senses' (*Groundwork of the Metaphysics of Morals*, 401 n. 2 (p. 69n. in H. J. Paton's translation, New York: Harper & Row, 1964). This passage supports a reading of the quotation above which emphasises the end of it, with its view of respect as a feeling which is a by-product of being rationally motivated.

Kant explains his understanding of respect for people in a long footnote in the *Groundwork*, the crucial point of which is:

> The object of respect is, therefore, nothing but the law . . .
> All respect for a person is properly only respect for the law
> (of honesty, etc.) of which the person provides an
> example.[12]

In respecting people we merely respect the law which they exemplify. It is not clear what this respect entails in practice. Be that as it may, this Kantian respect for people is not the respect that is due to people as people, or as persons.[13] In fact it is not really respect even for people who obey the moral law because they obey the moral law. It is respect for the moral law which those who obey it exemplify in their conduct. Consider an analogy: people who love the sea may love sea paintings, because they depict the sea. If they are not otherwise lovers of paintings their love of sea paintings may be not a love of them as good paintings, not even as good sea paintings. Rather, they love them as mementoes of the sea. Kant's language suggests an analogous relation between respect for people who obey the moral law and respect for the moral law: the people are illustrations of the moral law which is respected by respecting its illustrations.[14]

---

[12] *Groundwork*, sec. 402n.

[13] Note that one need not be guilty of moral transgressions to fail to qualify for Kantian respect. One may be a person who always acts according to the moral law, but never for the moral law.

[14] Interestingly, this is the relationship which exists according to some religions between a god or a saint and a sacred representation of, or relic of, them.

The influence of Kant's moral philosophy on contemporary discussions of personal moral respect derives from the fact that Kant's own use of the notion of 'respect for persons' did not always conform to his explanation of it. In particular, he used it in the context of his doctrine that people are ends in themselves, and his discussion of the imperative that in all one's actions one must treat people's humanity not merely as a means but as an end as well.

> [R]ational beings are called persons inasmuch as their nature already marks them out as ends in themselves, i.e., as something which is not to be used merely as means and hence there is imposed thereby a limit on all arbitrary use of such beings, which are thus objects of respect.[15]

The two grounds of respect (i.e., people exemplifying the moral law by following it, and people being ends in themselves) are quite different, and could lead to different reasons for action. However, for Kant the two converge, so that the slippage of meaning is easy to overlook. If the moral law consists of the requirement to treat others not only as means, but also as ends in themselves, then in respecting the moral law we respect others. Here we respect persons not because they exemplify the moral law in their conduct, but because we ought to treat them as ends in themselves. Respect for persons (in this second sense) is the same as treating people (or rather their humanity) as ends in themselves.

Darwall in his influential article 'Two kinds of respect'[16] identifies Kant's use of respect for persons in this second

---

[15] *Groundwork*, 428.
[16] *Ethics*, 88 (1977), 36 at 46.

sense with his own explanation of what he calls 'recognition-respect' for persons:

> To have recognition respect for someone as a person is to give appropriate weight to the fact that he or she is a person by being willing to constrain one's behaviour in ways required by that fact . . . Recognition respect for persons, then, is identical with recognition respect for the moral requirements that are placed on one by the existence of other persons.[17]

Following Darwall, Frankena explains that 'in effect, to respect persons in this sense is just to regard them as morally

---

[17] *Ibid.* S. L. Darwall multiplies unnecessarily types of respect. The difference between appraisal-respect and recognition-respect in his article is not between two kinds of respect but between two types of objects of respect, each respected in the way appropriate to it. This is easily obscured from view by the fact that 'I respect this person' does not disclose what I respect him as. I can respect him as a moral person, or as a dedicated teacher – which are cases of Darwallian appraisal-respect, or respect as a person, or as the president of the United States – cases of Darwallian recognition-respect. It is true that my respect for him as a moral person and my respect for him as a person manifest themselves in different attitudes and actions. But so do my respect for him as a moral person and my respect for him as a teacher. In each case the ways my respect manifests itself differ depending on its object and grounds. Such differences do not amount to showing that there are radically different kinds of respect, one being recognition, the other appraisal respect.

    If this is correct then we are left without a clarification of the concept of respect. Once we merge appraisal and recognition respect the generic notion becomes something like: recognising the value of the object of respect, and being disposed to react appropriately. But this explanation is too wide. I will return to this point below. For the purpose of our argument we can rely on our unarticulated understanding of respect.

considerable as such'.[18] That means 'that a person's existence as such makes it wrong or bad to treat her or him in some ways and right or good to do so in others'.[19]

We respect people as people when recognising that there are limitations on the way one may impact on persons, limitations derived from the fact that they are persons. One respects persons, one does not treat them as a means only, but also as ends, one treats persons as members of the kingdom of ends, if one treats them as persons should be treated.

All this may sound platitudinous. It includes the important point that respecting people is a way of treating them. It is neither a feeling, nor an emotion, nor a belief, though it may be based on a belief and be accompanied (at least occasionally) by certain feelings. It is a way of conducting oneself, and more indirectly, of being disposed to conduct oneself towards the object of the respect. Beyond this point, however, is not the idea of treating persons as persons should be treated platitudinous? We should treat cars as cars should be treated, computers as computers should be treated, and persons as persons should be treated. How else? Perhaps the difference is this: stating that persons should be treated as persons should be treated implies that there is a way persons qua persons should be treated, and that suggests that some intrinsic properties of persons have the consequence that they should be treated in a certain way. Perhaps this means that there are ways persons should be treated just because they are persons, independently

[18] 'The Ethics of Respect for Persons', 157.
[19] *Ibid.*

of all else.[20] That may be taken to mean that the reason is un-conditional on anything, that it would persist however much the rest of the world changes. Alternatively, it may mean that the ground for the reason involves nothing else, that its intel-ligibility can be established without reference to anything else. The features whose presence is all that is needed to establish the intelligibility of a claim that there is a reason to V can be called a complete reason (to V). Let us assume that stating that one should treat people as people should be treated implies that the presence of some intrinsic properties of persons is a reason which is both (a) unconditional, and (b) complete for a certain way of treating persons. The same is not true of advice to respect cars or computers. Here the reason to respect them is their use to oneself or others. Being due to their instrumental value, it arises out of their non-intrinsic, that is, extrinsic prop-erties rather than arising from limitations on treating them in virtue of being what they are in themselves.

What intrinsic property or properties of people con-stitute a complete and unconditional reason for treating them with respect? And what mode of treating people would sat-isfy the requirement to treat them with respect? The Kantian thought is that the answer to the first question is in the fact that persons are (necessarily or essentially) ends in themselves. To examine this suggestion we need first to understand what it is to be an end in itself, and then an explanation of why there is a reason to treat what is an end in itself with respect.

---

[20] This does not entail that such reason is overriding or has any specific strength.

3 On being an end in itself

We need a formal characterisation of what it is to be an end in itself, one which will not depend directly on identifying special cases of ends in themselves, but will merely identify what is the difference between ends in themselves and other ends. Such a characterisation will enable us to examine the question whether persons are ends in themselves, and whether there could be other such ends.[21]

One such characterisation is offered by Nozick:

> Side constraints upon action reflect the underlying
> Kantian principle that individuals are ends and not merely
> means . . . There is no side constraint on how we may use a
> tool, other than the moral constraints on how we may use
> it upon others . . . there is no limit on what we may do to it
> to best achieve our goals. Now imagine that there was an
> overrideable constraint C on some tool's use. For example,
> the tool might have been lent to you only on the condition
> that C not be violated unless the gain from doing so was
> above a certain specified amount, or unless it was
> necessary to achieve a certain specified goal. Here the
> object is not *completely* your tool, for use according to your
> wish or whim. But it is a tool nevertheless, even with
> regard to the overrideable constraint. If we add constraints
> on its use that may not be overridden, then the object may
> not be used as a tool *in those ways. In those respects*, it is not

---

[21] For reasons I will not discuss here, I agree with those who do not find Kant's own development of these ideas entirely satisfactory. Hence the following exploration follows different paths, albeit paths which are Kantian in spirit, at least to a degree.

> a tool at all. Can one add enough constraints so that an
> object cannot be used as a tool at all, in *any* respect?[22]

This line of thinking, echoing Kant's language cited above, is
not without appeal. If we are restricted in what we can do with
an object, for reasons other than its current or future use for
us, then that restriction cannot derive from the fact that it is a
tool. It follows that there is some normatively relevant aspect
to it which is not accounted for by its being a tool. It is not, we
could say, merely a tool. Similarly it is not entirely given to our
use, since there are reasons to treat it this way or that that do
not arise from the use we have or may have for it. But does it
follow that it is an end in itself?

Nozick seems to think that if we cannot use it as a
tool in any way at all then it is an end in itself. But this must
be a mistake. As Kant implies, what is an end in itself may
also have a value for others, and there is nothing wrong in
them pursuing their interests in it, so long as in doing so they
respect its standing as an end in itself. Nozick's characterisation
is exclusive: an object has the standing of an end to the extent
that it is not a means to anything.

The main difficulty with Nozick's approach is that he
assumes that not being allowed to treat an object as a tool is
tantamount to treating it as an end in itself. We can take Nozick
to imply not only that we, that is, each one of us, cannot use the
object as we wish (this may be for no other reason than that it is
useful as a tool to someone else), but that there are limitations
on the way it ought to be dealt with which do not derive from

[22] *Anarchy, State and Utopia* (New York: Basic Books, 1974), pp. 30–1.

its instrumental value to anyone (i.e., that the limits on its use by each of us do not derive merely from its instrumental value to others). Even so, the conclusion is merely that the object has non-instrumental, that is, intrinsic value. It does not follow that it is an end in itself.

First, not every act which does not treat an object as a means to an end treats it as an end in itself. Purposeless acts, such as expressive acts, are a case in point. When kicking the table in exasperation one is not using the table as a means to an end, nor treating it as an end in itself. To think that one is using the table as a means to express one's exasperation is to confuse expressive action with action designed to express or relieve an emotion.[23]

Purposeless actions do not contain restrictions on the use of an object. It would be a mistake, however, to think that the existence of a rationally justified restriction on the use of an object which does not derive from its use-value shows that it is an end in itself. A simple illustration is provided by one common, and correct,[24] view of good works of art. They are to be valued in themselves, and therefore there are restrictions on their use which do not derive from their instrumental value to anyone. These are restrictions arising out of the intrinsic value of good works of art, which is why they deserve our respect.

[23] Perhaps some irrational actions are clearer examples. It is possible, however, to avoid their force by limiting the thesis to rational actions, on the ground that by their nature, irrational actions are liable to be an exception to many general theses about action.

[24] For our purpose its correctness does not matter, so long as it is acknowledged that it could be a correct view of works of art or of some other objects.

The point is not that even good works of art are not as valuable as persons. Perhaps some works of art are more valuable than some persons. At least it may be rational to expect people to risk or sacrifice their life to create or preserve great works of art. The point is that persons, even if they have instrumental value, and even if they are valuable in the same ways that all intrinsically valuable objects (such as good works of art) are, are *also* valuable in a different way. We now see that having value in virtue of an intrinsic feature is not sufficient to characterise being an end in itself. It is this difference between the various kinds of value that their intrinsic properties may endow things with that we need to understand.

There is another difficulty with Nozick's statement quoted above. It assumes that for the tool to be an end in itself the non-tool-related reasons must be absolute, that is, ones which cannot be overridden. That is consistent with the Kantian view of respecting people, but may be controversial, and it would be better to have an explanation which has this feature, if at all, as its consequence, rather than as one of its defining features. That is, it would be better if we could use the account of ends in themselves to motivate the absolute character of the reason to respect, when it has such a character.

This leads to a wider point: Nozick's statement suggests[25] that it is possible to explain the nature of ends in themselves by the character of the treatment of whatever is an end in itself. This, however, abandons the thought that one's being an end in oneself is the *ground* for being treated in the

---

[25] And given its brevity it is difficult to know how much one is entitled to read into it. Is it just an informal illustration rather than a characterisation as I am treating it here?

appropriate way. To be that, one needs a characterisation of being an end in oneself which is at least partly independent of the way ends in themselves should be treated. Perhaps, however, the etymology suggests otherwise: to say of something that it is an end in itself may be to say that it should be treated as an end, but not for the sake of any further end beyond it. That is, the expression suggests how to treat something, rather than specifying a ground for so treating it.

This only gives rise to another difficulty: it is far from clear in what way a person can be an end, either in itself or any other way. I can make it my end to get people jobs, or to see to it that they come to no harm, or to ensure them a comfortable income, or to keep them from temptation, and so on. But can they themselves, rather than securing them something, be my ends? I think that we tend to equate being an end in itself with being of value in oneself, and take that condition as a ground for a certain treatment, that is, with respect. Let us therefore examine the notion of being of value in oneself, borrowing the points already made, that is, that that would involve having intrinsic features which endow one with unconditional value, where that value is independent of being good for something or someone else, and its possession is a complete reason for treating its possessor with respect.[26]

---

[26] Frances Kamm's discussion of people as ends in themselves in *Morality, Mortality*, vol. II, *Rights, Duties and Status* (Oxford: Oxford University Press, 1996), is instructive: at no point does she try to explain how people could be *ends*, let alone ends in themselves. She takes the expression as a term of art, and I think that it is fair to say that her discussion is really of people as having value in themselves.

4 On being valuable in oneself

The concept of *being valuable in oneself* is a philosophical concept. It emerged to mark a certain category of value whose existence is established by the very nature of value, that is, if anything is of value at all then something is valuable in itself. We understand the concept if we understand its role relative to other essential value concepts. The concepts on which I will comment are all of things having value, or being good. Two initial caveats will help avert misunderstandings. First, my inflationary use of value, explained, and justified, in chapter 2 above, will be followed here as well. Any property possession of which necessarily can explain and justify performing acts which possess it, acquiring objects, or entering or persevering in relationships which have it, etc., is a value property, one which necessarily renders whatever possesses it *pro tanto* good. Properties possession of which inherently justifies or makes intelligible avoidance, etc., indicate that their possessors are, *pro tanto*, bad. They are bad-making properties. Second, we need to distinguish between categorical and relational propositions about the goodness of things. My concern is with propositions of the form 'x is good (or "of value")', and not with propositions of the form 'y is good for (or "has value for") x'. Propositions of the form 'y is good for x' can be true even though the corresponding proposition 'x is good' is false. 'More information will be good for the conspiracy' does not imply that the conspiracy is good.

It is inherent in the nature of value that whatever is valuable is either valuable for something or someone of value,

or is valuable in itself.[27] Clearly, whatever is valuable instrumentally, that is, because of its consequences, or likely consequences, or (as with things, like tools, which are means to ends)
because of the use which can be made of it, is so valuable because of its contribution to something else which is valuable.[28]
The same is also true of most intrinsic goods. Good works
of art, friendships, games of tennis (when all these are judged
apart from their instrumental value), are valuable because they
can be good for people.

Whenever one thing is valuable or good for another[29]
we can explain how it is so. Replacing engine oil is good for
engines for it makes them function better, in specifiable ways.
Replacing the water in the vase is good for the flowers because

---

[27] Hence while 'y is good for x' does not imply 'x is good', the latter, I claim,
implies either 'there is something good that x is good for', or 'x is good in
itself'. I am relying in the next few paragraphs on my analysis of these
matters in 'The Amoralist' in *Engaging Reason*.

[28] This point is often overlooked. It is often assumed that something is
instrumentally good just if there is something for which it is good,
however valueless, or even bad, that thing is. But if something is
instrumentally valuable it is valuable. It is worth having, or keeping or
acquiring, or it has exchange value, etc. But if all that can be said for it is
that there is something it is good for, e.g., that it is good for making
people suffer, it does not follow that it is good. Indeed, as in this
example, it may well be bad.

[29] Like the rest of the observations about the use or meaning of various
expressions made here, the comments about 'good for' are not meant to
be an accurate, let alone a comprehensive account of the use of the
expression. They are meant to capture a central, or core use of it. But it is
worth observing that they apply to 'good for a thing (or for things)', not
'good for an action' (e.g., 'this knife is good for torturing').

it makes them look attractive for longer. Inoculating the cat is good for it for it protects it from illness, etc. The explanation often points to, or presupposes, that what the good is good for is itself good because it is, or can be, good for someone or something else. Changing the oil is good for the engine, because a well-functioning engine is good for . . . . However, this chain has to stop somewhere for any of its links to make sense at all. The conditional[30] must come to rest with some unconditional good, we might say. Otherwise it will all be good for nothing. Whatever is good unconditionally is good in itself.

This is not an observation about infinite regress. Not every infinite regress defies intelligibility. It is an observation about the nature of value. If A is good for B which is itself devoid of value, that A is good for B is no reason for anyone to do anything, nor a reason for valuing A in any way at all. It is as if A's value is without value. In other words it, A, is without value. If B is good, but only inasmuch as it is or can be good for C, then whether the value of A means anything (as explained above) depends on whether C is valuable. If A is watering or spraying a protective spray on B, which is a plant – which is good because it enables B to produce C, its fruit – then the value of watering or spraying A depends on whether the fruit is of any value (assuming that B is not valuable in any other way). If there is nothing good in the fruit, what good is watering it?

---

[30] We use the contrast between a 'conditional' and an 'unconditional' good relative to different possible conditions in different contexts. Here 'a conditional good' is conditioned on (a) being good for something or someone, which is (b) also good or of value.

The argument is not deductive and its conclusion not without exception. The exceptions are of familiar kinds. For example, we will find discourse about what is good where the truth of statements about the value of things is determined by what some people or doctrines of faith or others take to be good. There may be domains of discourse reflecting the beliefs of previous generations which are used without their normative significance now, much in the way in which religious terminology permeates secular discourse, having lost its religious meaning, in the way in which I use the word 'creature' without assuming the existence of a creator.

That what is good is either good in itself or is capable of being good for something else does not reduce all that is not good in itself to the status of an instrumental good. When one says that reading Proust enriches one's life one is not pointing to the consequences of the reading. Rather reading Proust with understanding is such enrichment. Engaging with intrinsic goods in the right way and with the right spirit (and both way and spirit differ for a tennis match and for Proust) is good for one in and of itself, in one of many possible ways.

Similarly, that whatever is not good in itself is good only if it can be good for someone or something does not mean that what *makes* it good is that it can be good for someone or something. Intrinsic goods differ here from instrumental goods. For instrumental goods the inference is valid: what makes a good car good is that it can be used by people. But the inference fails for intrinsic goods. What makes Bonnard's *The Garden* a good painting is its sumptuous colour, its dense colouristic texture, its success in portraying the depth of the garden and its plants in spite of its apparent flatness, its use of this flatness to disguise and ambiguate spatial relations, etc. It is good for us because it is good, not good because it is good for us. Yet it would not be good unless it could be good for us (or for someone else, some extra-terrestrials, etc.). The way that being capable of being good for us constrains the features which can make it good is indirect. Potential relevance for human life is built into the criteria for art, and for being a successful work of art. The success of an individual work of art is then determined by its success as a work of art.

Whatever is not good in itself is good only if it can be good for someone or something else. Is there also a reverse dependence? Must it be the case that if someone or something is good in itself then there is something or someone which can be good for it? At first blush the suggestion may be surprising. After all, the argument for the existence of goods in themselves was that otherwise nothing will be of any 'real' value. To make sense of the possibility of value one needs to anchor value in what is unconditionally valuable. How can the value of what is unconditionally valuable be conditioned by the possibility of there being things which are only conditionally valuable? Yet such mutual dependence is possible, and need not be symmetrical. If the way the unconditional depends on the conditional differs from the way the conditional depends on the unconditional the asymmetry indicated by the contrast between conditional and unconditional can be preserved.

The reverse dependence is presupposed in the common understanding of value. We do assume that what is of value in itself can interact with others or other things in a beneficial or detrimental way. What would it be to deny that? It would require belief in the possibility of a strong form of value autarchy. If a mountain of indestructible material, for example, totally stable non-reactive, non-meltable, etc., gold, were valuable in itself then the reverse dependence would not apply to it: there will be nothing which is good for it. It cannot interact with anything in a way beneficial to it. It is just there. The thought that what is of value in itself can be like that is puzzling. We assume that what is of value in itself must have a life, or a history, that is, that it is capable of interacting in meaningful ways with others or with other things, through which it thrives or declines. On the assumption that everything in the natural world causally interacts with other parts of the natural world, the supposition of such an autarchic thing is nearly impossible. It is not literally impossible because only interactions which affect the value of the thing or its history are relevant to this form of autarchy. But given that duration is likely to be a good in what is a good in itself, it is reasonable to suppose that autarchy is impossible, and this would help to explain why our understanding of value seems to rule it out.[31]

I will assume that by its nature value presupposes a mutual dependence. Whatever is good or of value (at least

---

[31] If there were an autarchic good in itself, disproving the mutual dependence thesis, it would be difficult to establish that this is so. Presumably if it were known to us we would admire or value it, and such a valuing would be good for us (see on this below). But then what is supposed to be good in itself would also be good for us, for we would be better for knowing it, admiring it, etc. It would therefore be also an intrinsic good. What would establish that it is not only an intrinsic good but also a good in itself? From our perspective this may be a distinction without a difference.

unless it is a good in itself[32]) can be good for, or of value to, someone or something, a chain ending with beings good in themselves. The goodness of, or the history, or life, of what is good in itself requires being affected by or engaging in the appropriate way with what is good for it.

5 On the value of valuers

It is time we moved from reflecting on the abstract category of being of value in itself, to the question of who or what is of such value? I will pursue the question only as it applies to people, though the pattern of argument to be used would serve without restriction.

If anything has value then things can exist which are of value in themselves. For it is of the nature of whatever is of value but not valuable in itself that its value presupposes that it can be good for, or of value to, something else, and ultimately to what is of value in itself. While nothing of value in itself need exist at any given time, such things must be capable of existing for that possibility is a precondition of anything being valuable but not valuable in itself being even possible.

To show of anything valuable that it is of value in itself it is sufficient to establish that (a) there are things which are good for it,[33] but (b) their being good for it is not conditional on

---

[32] I will argue below that what is good in itself can also be good for others than itself. The bracketed exception is not a real exception.

[33] Is that the same as making it, or its life (history) better? Probably not. But this shows how I have been overusing the notion of 'good for'. In a natural reading of it the answer to the question is affirmative. However, I have been using 'good for' as equivalent to 'would be a good thing for the

it contributing to the good of something else.[34] This criterion relies on one aspect of the more general point that something good is good in itself if its being good is not conditional on anything else being good.[35]

A common, and Kantian (though not exclusively so), view has it that people are of value in themselves because they are valuers. This seems to me right, but before we examine some reasons supporting this view, a couple of clarifications. First, I am not claiming that only valuers are of value in themselves. That they are the only ones is, of course, a common, and a Kantian, view. It sometimes leads people in the direction of an ethics of reciprocity, of ethics as the shared obligations of and towards moral agents.[36] I will not make any such assumption. Most likely members of many other animal species who are not moral agents are also ends in themselves,[37] valuable in themselves, and there may be others.

---

agent to do or have, etc.'. It is, other things being equal, good for me to have this ice cream now. It does not follow that it will make my life, let alone me, better to have it.

[34] Note that this condition is not met by intrinsic goods, such as good works of art, whose value depends on the fact that they are good for people, in the rather loose or broad understanding of 'good for' in which I use the expression.

[35] In that sense things which are good because they can be good for someone or something else are conditionally good. Their goodness is conditional on the possibility of the existence of other goods, the goods that they can be good for.

[36] See for example C. Korsgaard, 'The Reasons We Can Share' in *Altruism*, ed. Ellen Frankel Paul, Fred D. Miller, Jr., and Jeffrey Paul (New York: Cambridge University Press, 1993).

[37] Though at least some of them may also be valuers in the relevant sense.

Second, my understanding of valuers is much more relaxed, and extensive, than that of many writers, including Kant. It encompasses all natural creatures capable of intentional action.[38] Intentional action is action for reasons, that is, action undertaken in light of an appreciation of oneself and one's circumstances. It is a response to the (perceived) normative aspects of the world as they relate to one. That is why agents (i.e., those capable of intentional action) are valuers. But such valuation may only be implicit, or below the level of consciousness. It need include no more than recognition that a course of action will be painful, or pleasurable.[39] But it must include recognition of such facts as reasons (though not necessarily through use of these concepts). It must consist of directing one's conduct and one's life, in light of one's understanding of those features of the world which are reasons, rather than merely reflex-responses to factors which are in fact reasons. I am not assuming that there is a sharp divide between valuers and non-valuers.

Why are valuers of value in themselves? The argument I will give here has three parts. The first relies on the mutual

[38] Many manmade, or culturally generated, agents meet the condition of being evaluators. I do not think that they are of value in themselves. They are, in a sense which remains to be explained, evaluators derivatively only. But I will not discuss their standing here.

[39] That is, valuers may have to be capable of recognising that options fall under this or that evaluative concept (though the range of evaluative concepts they are capable of applying may be limited). But they need not be able to master concepts such as 'options', 'evaluative concepts', nor to have thorough mastery even of the evaluative concepts that they have some grasp of.

but asymmetrical dependence of intrinsic goods which are good for someone and those which are unconditionally good, that is, good in themselves. Evaluative thought, I argued, presupposes both types of valuable things and creatures. The tacit assumption there was that what is good for someone is there to be engaged with in the right way.[40] In a way, intrinsic values are there to be engaged with by those who are of value in themselves. Their value is realised when those of value in themselves engage with them in the right way.

The use of 'realised' may mislead, and suggest that they are not of value until realised. Perhaps novels which are unread are of only potential value. That, however, is a mistake, and is not true to our concepts of value and of the good. It does, however, admit of the possibility that the value of things which are of actual, not merely potential, value will be wasted. That is what the reference to realised values was meant to convey. Goods whose value is realised are not wasted goods. All this is a bit of a mouthful to say that paintings are there to be seen and appreciated, novels to be read, oranges to be eaten, mountains to be looked at, or climbed, etc. They are there for these things to happen to them in the sense that their value to others remains unrealised until someone of value in himself relates to them in the right way.

---

[40] This crucial notion resists quick general explanation. What is the right way to engage with a good depends on the kind of good it is. If it is a novel it would be to read it with understanding and interest, if a tennis game – to be absorbed by the game, and display skill in playing it, etc. Often the expression 'engage in it in the right way' is inappropriately inflated: does eating an orange require eating it slowly while enjoying its fragrance, juicy texture, and taste?

Valuing something of value, recognising its value, is a paradigm of engaging with what is valuable in the right way. Sometimes it is nearly the only element of such engagement. In listening to music, watching ballet, reading novels or poems, looking at paintings, and so on, appreciating what one hears or sees, recognising, more or less fully, its value in its various aspects, when done with due attention and understanding, and without resentment or envy, etc., is the right way to engage with such works of art.[41] In other cases recognising the value of what one is engaged with is only part, but an essential part, of the right mode of engagement with value. When climbing a mountain or playing tennis, or representing a client in court, or designing a building, much more is involved than recognition. But without understanding the potential value of what one is doing, and thereby the difference between doing it well and failing to do it well, without such an understanding one's engagement with the valuable activity is defective.

Some people maintain that recognition of value is a necessary element in any proper engagement with any intrinsic value (though of course what that recognition involves differs greatly, from the appreciation of a fresh slice of bread, to the

---

[41] The example illustrates that recognition of value is more than a belief that the thing is of value, more even than a belief that it has the specific value that it does in fact have. Listening to music with attention and understanding, etc., is not entailed by mere belief in the value of the music. It presupposes such a belief, but consists of much more, it consists of congeries of attitudes and responses appropriate to that value. To be a valuer, as the concept is here understood, is to be capable of recognising value, of valuing what is valuable, and not merely being able to form beliefs about the value of things.

appreciation of Proust). Arguably it is a mark of an intrinsic value that it cannot contribute to a person or a life without being recognised for the value it is. This bald statement would require much qualification to be true of all people and of other animals which can benefit from intrinsic goods. The case of sensual pleasures illustrates the limitations on the statement. In any case, recognition of the value of what is valuable is at least part of many forms of engagement with value in the right way. Those capable of it, that is, those we called valuers, therefore, meet the first condition of being a good in itself. If there are intrinsic values whose realisation requires recognition, a recognition which being valuers they can give, then there are things, which are, assuming that the valuers are good, good for them.

To show that valuers not only play the role of being of value in themselves in relation to goods which are good for others, but that they actually are of value in themselves one has, secondly, to show that their good does not matter simply because it is a good for someone or something else. People may be of value in themselves even if they are of value to others, so long as their value or the value of their life is not due solely to the fact that they are of value to others. When I think of the different things which are intrinsically good for people, and which their ability to recognise value enables them to engage in, I cannot think of a way in which being enriched by values in many of these ways can be accounted for by the use that people may be to others. Mostly when people are of use to others they are of use to other people, and that does not help in showing that people are not of value in themselves. For the most part it shows no more than that what is good for us can often be shared, and shared in ways which enhance its value for all those for whom it is good.

The way people are of use to other animals often displays the same pattern, of shared goods, whose sharing enhances their value to those who share them. When our value to animals and other things fails this test it also fails to relate to most of the values which enrich people's lives. The appreciation of the arts, of sports, of the pleasures of fashion or of gourmet food, provides but a few examples which seem wholly or almost entirely unrelated to any use people may be to animals of other species. Hence as valuers people not only fill the role of what is of value in itself, but they do so as the ultimate link in the chain, and not because they are good for something else only.

The final part of the argument has to explain why filling that role in relations of value makes people of value in themselves not only when they engage with value, but even when they do not. At this point the argument is simple: the very idea of something which is of value in itself is the idea of someone who *can* relate to value in the appropriate way. In a world of objects with duration the notion singles out some by their potential relation to value. Just as the fact that an object has intrinsic value marks a potential in it, the potential of being engaged with in the right way, so the status of being someone of value in oneself marks a potential in one, the potential to engage with value in the right way, and be thereby enriched or improved, etc. Therefore, valuers are of value in themselves.

But cannot one forfeit the standing of being of value in oneself if one fails to engage with value in the right way, or if one chooses worthless, debased, or wrongful options? The worry is misguided. It is crucial to the status of being an end it itself that it marks a potential, not its realisation. One is of value in oneself if there can be things which are good for one, and not merely because one serves the interests of others. The standing is not jeopardised just because one does not engage with what is good for one, as one should. Such a failure is indeed significant. It warrants and even requires certain attitudes and actions towards such failures, and towards the people whose failure it is. They should feel disappointed, ashamed, etc., and others would react similarly. However, these reactions can only be appropriate when directed at people who are ends in themselves, and do not show that they have lost this status.

6 Introducing reasons of respect

The explanation I offered of the nature of what is of value in itself, and the argument to show that valuers are of value in themselves, may disappoint. They are technical and structural. They do not resemble ethical arguments about the value of anything. We may ask: if that is why people are of value in themselves why does one have to respect them or anything else which has such value? There is another way of raising the same question: if that is what it means to be of value in itself then being so is just a fact (albeit an evaluative one) of theoretical interest: for example, it expresses the division of valuables into conditional and unconditional. But why should that theoretically significant fact be a reason for anything more? Could it possibly constitute, or be the ground for, a reason to respect people because they are good in themselves?

Let me start with one aspect of the answer: respecting people is good for those who respect them. That means that in

158

being of value in themselves people are also intrinsically good, that is good for other people. How so? It is easy to point to many ways in which people are good for others. The whole of human culture depends on it. That people are valuers, presupposes that they can understand their surroundings and themselves. They form attitudes, emotions, intentions, and beliefs in light of their appreciation of their circumstances, in light of their understanding of the normative significance of aspects of their situation. That ability is the basis of so many of the goods available to themselves, but also to other people. People share in the creation of objects of value, share in the creation of, and engagement in, intrinsically valuable practices and relationships. Friendship, common engagement in community and social affairs, literature and the arts, are among the many goods illustrating this point. They are created by people in ways which make them and their activities valuable to others. Obviously, people are good for other people (though, needless to say, they can also be bad for them), and they are so because they are valuers.

This is, however, much less than we are looking for when we are looking for the foundations of a duty of respect – or is it? Our notion of a duty of respect, even when it is not conceived as the foundation of the whole of morality, is of a duty which we owe to all human beings in equal degree. Perhaps this is an illusion, or a result of a misconception, but unless we are to reject the thought that we owe a general duty of respect to other human beings at all, the revisions must be fairly marginal. Possibly we do not owe a duty of respect to the terminally comatose, or to psychopathic murderers, or there may be other exceptions. At least it may be that we do not owe them the same duty, or do not owe it with the same stringency, as we owe others generally. Exceptions aside, the duty – as normally conceived – would not admit of too much modulation to trace the different ways in which some people are, while others are not, or are less, good for us.

The point is valid, but it is no objection to seeking the ground for respect in the fact that people are of value in themselves, and therefore of value to others. It only shows that the duty of respect cannot be grounded in the particular ways in which people are of value for one another. It does not show that their being of value in themselves, and therefore, their being in general of value to one another, or, if you like, capable of being of value to one another, cannot be the ground of respect.

Remember that respect in general is a species of recognising and being disposed to respond to value, and thereby to reason.[42] In what way is the notion of respect narrower than that? Consider the different ways we can react to the work of Michelangelo. My recognition of the value of the works can lead me to travel to distant churches and museums in order to spend time contemplating them, studying them and the circumstances and the process of their creation, and much else. I could draw them, derive inspiration from them in my own

[42] As usual, I discuss good-making properties, expecting that the conclusions apply, *mutatis mutandis*, to bad-making properties. It is interesting, however, to note an asymmetry between them. We ought to respect what is intrinsically valuable, inasmuch as it is valuable, and we should not respect the bad, inasmuch as it is bad. Nor should we respect what was bad in that it led to bad consequences. But, we should respect what has a power to produce bad, as well as what has the power to do good. Respecting the potential of things to produce bad consequences is just being wary of their power and/or propensity to do ill.

work, try to buy them to have them in my possession, and so on. None of these activities would it be natural to attribute to a motive of respect. Respect for Michelangelo's work consists primarily in acknowledging his achievement in what we say, and think, and in caring about the preservation of the work. This fact reflects another: one need not be an art connoisseur to respect Michelangelo's work, nor need one be among those who spend time examining it and admiring it. Not everyone need be an art connoisseur, or a devotee of Michelangelo's work. But everyone ought to respect his work.

We can generalise from this example. Without regarding the classification as hard and fast, we could distinguish three stages of correct response to value, and to the presence of good-making properties in objects. First, and at the most basic level, comes appropriate psychological acknowledgement of value, that is, regarding objects in ways consistent with their value, in one's thoughts, understood broadly to include imaginings, emotions, wishes, intentions, etc. I do not mean to imply that we should believe that whatever is of value is of value. There is no general reason to know, or believe, that what is of value is of value, any more than there is a general reason to know or to believe in all true propositions. No reason for me to believe that there is in Kazakhstan a good statue of the Buddha, even though there is such a statue there. But there is a general reason that if we think of an object which is of value, we should think of it in ways consistent with its value. This applies to our fantasies, imaginings, wishes, emotions, as well as to our plain beliefs. For example, despising someone as worthless, or mean, when he is in fact generous and kind, is having an emotion inconsistent with his value, and inconsistent with the general reason I have in mind here: the reason that in our thoughts we regard objects in ways consistent with the value they in fact have.

Given the close relation of thought to its expression in language and other symbolic actions I will regard expression of recognition of value in language and other symbolic actions as also belonging with the first stage of relating to value.

Second, there is a general reason to preserve what is of value. Naturally, the strength of the reason varies with the value of the object. But in general we have reason not to destroy, and furthermore, to preserve what is of value. There are difficult questions regarding the nature and limits of these reasons.[43] I will say nothing of them, except to assume that reasons of respect enjoin us not to destroy, and possibly to preserve, but not to create new objects of value.[44]

Third, we can engage with value in appropriate ways. We do so when we listen to music with attention and discrimination, read a novel with understanding, climb rocks using our

[43] For example, this reason gives way to the reasons there are for engaging in the value, or for using it in appropriate ways: it would be silly when hungry not to eat a banana in order not to destroy something of value, and we strive for a balance between preserving works of art and viewing them when this may lead to their deterioration.

[44] Suppose an expert carpenter builds a beautiful bookcase. She might have been at fault had she not done so. But she would not have shown lack of respect for that bookcase had she not made it. It is another question whether she may have shown lack of respect for herself or for the craft she mastered had she neglected it in general. My discussion here does not relate to these questions. They involve alleged duties to engage with objects of value, or in valuable activities. It is possible that sometimes such failure amounts to lack of respect for the value of the activity one neglects, or for oneself, in neglecting to lead a life of value.

skill to cope, spend time with friends in ways appropriate to our relationships with them, and so on and so forth.

The first two stages of relating to value contrast with the third. Ultimately, value is realised when it is engaged with. There is a sense in which music is there to be appreciated in listening and playing, novels to be read with understanding, friendships to be pursued, dances to be joined in, and so on. Merely thinking of valuable objects in appropriate ways and preserving them is a mere preliminary to engaging with value. Similarly, people are fulfilled, their virtues express themselves in their lives, and their lives are rewarding only if they engage with values in their lives. Merely not destroying or helping with the preservation of valuable objects, and thinking of them appropriately, is not enough for having a fulfilled life.[45] Yet, obviously no one has reason to engage with all valuable objects. We need not read all the novels, listen to all the music, climb all the mountains, go to all the parties, dance in all the dances, which are worthwhile. On the other hand, even though the first two stages are in a sense preparatory or preliminary only, they do involve reasons which apply to all. Not everyone has much time for Picasso's paintings, and there is nothing wrong in not caring for them (so long as it does not involve false beliefs about them or their value). But no one should destroy them, or treat them in ways inconsistent with the fact that they are

---

[45] This should be qualified to allow that one can have a fulfilling career as a conservator of objects of value of some kind or another. That is, one can make the preservation of valuable objects, or traditions, etc., one of one's main ways of engaging with value. There is no need here to develop the qualifications and details which show how this is consistent with the general view expressed in the text.

aesthetically valuable. No one need care for dancing. But no one should spoil (possibly other people's) dances. And so on.

The road I am pointing to is by now all too obvious. Reasons of respect are reasons belonging to the first two stages: reasons regarding the way we treat objects of value in thought and expression, and reasons for preserving them. These differ from reasons for engaging with valuable objects. But while in one way ultimately our lives are about engaging with value, the rest being mere preliminaries, in another way the reasons for respect are more basic. They are also more categorical, in not depending to the same degree on people's tastes and inclinations. Regarding what is of value, be it instrumental or intrinsic, there is a universal reason for everyone to respect it, which is the minimal form of engagement with value. It is the right reaction to what is of value even when you do not value it, you do not personally care for it. It is the form of recognising that a painting, a musical composition, a party, a friendship (other people's friendship), a game of chess (other people's game), are of value even though you do not wish to see the painting, listen to the music, join the party, and so on, for they are not your thing.

7 Why respect?

Why should this be so? And what is common to forms of respect? The case of respect is somewhat special. In general the value of what has value, and the action its value is a reason for, are intrinsically connected. We cannot understand what is of value in a party without understanding what it is a reason for, that is, when one has reason to go to one, and how one behaves at a party. Of course, this understanding is not very specific. First, because 'party' is a broad category, allowing for parties of many kinds. Understanding what the different kinds of parties are provides an understanding both of a more specific value or set of values and of more specific reasons to go, and how to do so. Second, the nature of (most) parties is such as to allow for spontaneous development. Understanding what parties are tells you that, but, on pain of being self-defeating, cannot tell you what will be made appropriate and what inappropriate by the spontaneous developments.

What goes for parties goes for musical compositions, mountaineering, philosophy, love, and everything else. There is no general recipe for determining what is the right way to engage with value. The good of what is of value determines for what conduct it provides reason, understanding the value depends on and leads to understanding the reason. How could it be otherwise? Consider the general problem: what can make it the case that a certain value is a reason for a certain action? Suppose that someone is painting his house green. When asked for his reason he says: 'I am painting it green because friendship has a great value' (or 'because my friendship with Jim is wonderful'). If the connection between the value of something and the action for which it is a reason is not arbitrary (and it cannot be arbitrary) then it must be determined by the value. That is, for the value of something to be a reason for an action it must determine what that action is, and it must be an essential property or aspect of what makes the valuable thing valuable which determines the action.

Suppose that it were not so, and that while the fact that X is V (has the good-making property V) is a reason to do A, that it is so is determined by something other than an essential aspect of X being V. If so, then X could be V without being a reason for A (i.e. in a situation where the determining property is absent).[46] Therefore it cannot be that X's being V is a reason to do A.[47] Indeed, given that the property which determines the action is not essentially related to X's being V there is nothing to suggest that it is X's being V rather than the determining property which is the reason for doing A.[48]

In saying that the value of what is of value determines what action, if any, it is a reason to perform, I do not mean to claim an epistemic priority of value over reasons for action. It is just as likely that our understanding of what is of value in something will derive from what it is a reason to do, as the other way round. Reason and value are inherently though asymmetrically connected. The main lesson for the present purpose is that there is no general formula determining what actions the value of what is of value provides reasons to perform. The

[46] I disregard the possibility that the determining property while not essential to X being V is necessarily present whenever X is V. Some further and fairly obvious argument will show that in all such variants it would be the determining property which is the reason, not X's being V.

[47] *Pace* the contrary position taken by Jonathan Dancy in *Moral Reasons* (Oxford: Blackwell, 1993). I argued against his view in *Engaging Reason*, chapter 10.

[48] Sometimes this fact is obscured from sight. For example, the good of baby-sitting for a friend seems only contingently connected to the reason for doing so, which is my promise to baby-sit. I would have had reason to do whatever (within limits) I promised to do. It just happened to be to baby-sit. My promise, however, is a reason to do whatever I promised. That is essential to the nature of a valid promise, and this valid promise is a promise to baby-sit, thus determining what I have reason to do, what would constitute the act of promise-keeping.

166

nature of the particular good determines what action it is a reason for, or, to use the terminology introduced above, what would be the appropriate way in which that good can be engaged with.

Not so with respect. There is a sense in which reasons of respect are not value-specific. There is one common ground to them all. Their precise boundaries may vary, as does their stringency. But their core is the same: if engaging with value is the way to realise value, respecting value is the way to protect the possibility of that realisation. The basic reasons that something being of value imposes are that it should be allowed to play its proper role, that is, that it should be allowed to be realised. This is particularly clear regarding the second stage, refraining from harming valuable things, and protecting them from damage.

The first stage of respect, recognition in thought and expression, contributes to maintaining attitudes which enable people to engage in value. This phase involves both individual and social aspects. On the one hand, in acknowledging that what is of value is of value in one's thought and expression one is holding oneself open to the possibility of engagement with value, even where one has no interest in doing so, and where one knows that one will never engage in it. On the other hand, in maintaining these attitudes oneself one is contributing to a social-cultural climate which makes engagement with these values conceivable and respectable. The very fact that things are of value requires at least that of us. As I explained above,[49] in themselves, and special circumstances apart, these reasons for respect, far from imposing sacrifices on people, contribute

[49] And in much greater detail in *Engaging Reason*.

167

to the value of their own life, as the pursuit of reason generally does.

Reasons for respect are categorical reasons, in the sense that their weight or stringency does not depend on our goals, tastes, or desires. Playing the piano, playing golf, teaching (professionally), spending the summer in Martinique, liking or admiring Dubuffet, or Cézanne, or Proust, being a friend of Jane, and most other things we have reason to do or be, and which give content to our lives, are all activities, relationships, attitudes, etc., which there are reasons to have, but the weight or stringency of these reasons depends on our tastes (if you do not have a taste for that kind of thing you will not benefit from it, and the reason to engage with it is very little) or goals (if you are seriously interested in the visual arts your reason to see the exhibition is much greater than mine), etc. Not so with reasons for respect: their stringency is not affected by our inclinations, tastes, goals, or desires. It does not follow that they are weightier, or more stringent than other reasons. Some are very stringent and others are less so, some of the other, non-categorical, reasons are among the most important in our life, others are among the most trivial. Yet, in being categorical reasons of respect are also reasons the flouting of which, when they predominate (that is when they defeat other reasons), is wrong. Acting against conclusive non-categorical reasons is usually foolish, unwise, or displays some other failing, and can be irrational, but is not wrong.[50]

---

[50] That helps to explain why reasons of respect are often associated with moral reasons. Yet in being reasons to respect whatever is of value their range is both wider and narrower than most conventional understandings of morality.

It has to be admitted that in appropriating the notion of respect to designate the general reasons one has to recognise the value of all that is of value even when one does not personally value it all, I am, while following a distinguished philosophical tradition, deviating from the ordinary ways in which the term is used. We do not often refer to respecting the value of cups and saucers, and when we do express our respect for the capacity of our enemies to harm us our meaning is not altogether captured by the explanations above. What matters is the distinction between the three stages of responding to value, and the fact that while taste has a lot to do with determining in which intrinsically valuable pursuits one will engage, the reasons for the responses of the first two stages are independent of taste and personal inclination. Given the direction of the debates about respect for people in ethics, it is appropriate to call them reasons for respect.

8 Respecting people

I think that we are making progress. But are we moving in the right direction? You may suspect that I have gone off the rails for instead of explaining respect for persons I am explaining respect for everything of value, including all instrumental values. How can anything remotely like respect for persons be derived from this? Surely, the respect we should manifest in our thought and action regarding the loaf of bread in the kitchen, if any, has nothing to do with respecting persons?

The doubt is understandable, but not justified. Respect for persons is just respect, as explained. What makes it different is that it applies to persons. How could it be respect for *people*, given that respect is for value, regardless of what value it is? It is and it is not. Its two aspects: acknowledging the value in word and deed, and preserving it, are products of nothing more than that the valuable is valuable. But what the acknowledgement consists in depends naturally on the content of the value, as do the actions required to preserve it. Similarly, the stringency of the reasons to acknowledge and preserve depends on the importance of the value. Not, let me remind you, its importance to any one valuer, but its importance as something which *can* be valued, value which *can* be realised.

This is why respecting people is relatively indifferent to how many love them, how creative they are, how much they contribute to humanity, etc. And this is why it is a more stringent duty than the one we have, in normal circumstances, towards a glass of water. This is also why it is less extensive than the duties of a friend, a lover, a parent, or an employer. They all value, or ought to value, the person they are so related to. The bulk of humanity need only respect him or her.

If respect for people differs from respect for works of art this is partly because the value of people differs from the value of works of art. It is also because people, unlike works of art, the comatose, and other animals have a sense of their own identity, a sense that they are of value, and therefore are hurt by disrespect, a fact which lends special stringency to duties of respect for people.[51] It also explains the special importance of

---

[51] Harry Frankfurt writes that treating a person disrespectfully, at least in matters of some consequence, 'may naturally evoke painful feelings of resentment. It may also evoke a more or less inchoate anxiety; for when a person is treated as though significant elements of his life count for nothing, it is natural for him to experience this as in a certain way an

symbolic acts of expressing respect. People who have a sense of their own value and understand when it is acknowledged and respected by others and when not can come greatly to resent disrespectful behaviour, and can come to expect affirmation of recognition of their value in symbolic manifestations of respect.

In this age where the politics of identity has acquired great prominence, we are particularly sensitive to symbolic expressions of respect. This very statement, however, obvious as it is, draws attention to one ambiguity in the previous paragraph. Is there 'a correct' degree of hurt which disregard of reasons for respect justifies, such that the stringency of reasons for respect is determined by it? Or is the stringency of these reasons determined by how much people are in fact hurt by disrespect, a matter surely contingent, and varying from individual to individual, but also from culture to culture?

In part the question is misconceived. Duties of respect for people require us to avoid causing the hurt which disrespect reasonably causes. But since, and to the extent that, we should avoid hurting people, we have reason (though not a reason of respect) to avoid conduct which will hurt through being

assault upon his reality. What is at stake for him, when people act as though he is not what he is, is a kind of self-preservation. It is not his biological survival that is challenged, of course, when his nature is denied. It is the reality of his existence for others, and hence the solidity of his own sense that he is real' ('Equality and Respect,' 153). As a description of people's psychological reactions this must be true of only some cases of violations of duty to respect people. But in describing the grounds for the alleged reactions his account chimes in with mine. A denial of the value of the person so treated, which is implied by the treatment, can be seen as an assault on his reality, when that does not mean his biological reality.

perceived as disrespectful, whether or not it is, and whether or not the hurt is reasonable, or proportionate to the offence.

But this is only part of the answer. I doubt whether the boundary between reasonable and unreasonable reactions to being treated disrespectfully can be drawn independently of (inherently variable) social practices in this matter. Social practices become relevant through the role of symbolic acts of respect, or disrespect. We tend to think of symbolic actions as those, like displaying flags, or singing anthems or other songs with symbolic meaning, or the use of respectful or disrespectful words (as modes of addressing people, etc.), which have only negligible non-symbolic effects. These I will call 'pure symbolic' acts. But acts which have other, 'real' significance to people can also become symbolic expressions of respect or disrespect. They are symbolic if they carry meaning because they are understood to have that meaning, rather than because of their 'real' consequences or significance, that is, meaning which they would have independently of their perceived meaning and significance. For example, having the vote in national elections is a matter of some importance, affecting the quality of government, and the likelihood that the interests of various groups in the country will be protected by governments. It has also come, quite naturally, to have a symbolic significance, so that not having the vote means being a second-class citizen: it is an expression of lack of respect for the individual.

As with most symbolic actions, including most purely symbolic actions, there are reasons why certain acts become symbolic of this or that. Giving flowers as presents (a purely symbolic act in our societies) is not unrelated to attitudes to flowers in our cultures, independently of their use as gifts or tokens. Having the vote, 'naturally' we are inclined to say, comes to have the symbolic meaning it has because of its instrumental function in facilitating the influence of people's interests on government policy. Moreover, commonly symbols do not come alone, but in interrelated webs. The symbolic significance of the vote is associated with the way we have come to think of membership (even the choice of this word is significant) in political communities (are they really communities? is not that just another symbolic expression of aspiration?). None of this should obscure the fact that seeing absence of the vote as signifying lack of respect is a result of the symbolic significance of the vote in our life.[52]

Symbolic acts of respect are theoretically interesting in that they show how a universal reason of respect for people leads to reasons for different acts in different cultures, for, of course, the meaning of social institutions and social practices can differ from one culture to another, an obvious enough point which is nevertheless often forgotten by some exponents of identity politics. Anything can come to be associated,

---

[52] More needs to be said to establish my point than can be done here. That young people or temporary visitors do not have the vote does not signify disrespect for them. Does that help establish that the association between respect and the vote is symbolic, being dependent on perceived meaning, not on its significance independently of such perceptions? Up to a point, but not entirely. One may try to associate the significance of the vote with a functional case for having it, for reasons for giving it, or denying it to people which are independent of its perceived meaning. If its purpose is to secure better government, granting it to temporary visitors or to young children may be counter-productive. To be sure, but my point is that even where it is functionally justified it need not be associated with respect or its absence. That connection is symbolic.

symbolically, with respect or disrespect for people. Naturally anything with bearing on people's interests can come to acquire such symbolic significance. Do reasons for respect always follow such symbolic, conventional, practices? Do we have reasons of respect to avoid any action which (symbolically) expresses disrespect in the circumstances in which it bears that meaning? Or could there be symbolic excesses in this matter? Can members of some societies, or of some groups within a society, come unreasonably to regard certain forms of conduct as an expression of disrespect?[53] The answer is probably complex: both can be the case. That is, it may be unreasonable or regrettable that some acts have the meaning they have, and yet while they have it, it may be disrespectful to perform them. Yet, in some circumstances the unreasonableness of taking acts to be expressions of disrespect may be such as to deny that they have that meaning.

All these, and other questions about the detailed scope and stringency of reasons of respect, are the questions which must be answered in order to understand the role of the doctrine of respect for people within the larger framework of morality.[54] Such explorations will have to await another occasion. Clearly I have barely begun to scratch the surface. I hope,

[53] Suppose that members of some religion came to regard the wearing of certain clothes, say of hats, as expressing disrespect for their members. Do we then have reasons of respect (as opposed to merely reasons to spare people's feelings) not to wear hats?

[54] Throughout the discussion I tried to bear in mind the lessons of Frankena's 'The Ethics of Respect for Persons', which successfully shows that one cannot regard duties of respect as the foundation of morality if that means that the rest of morality is no more than the working out of the implications of the doctrine of respect.

however, that enough has been said to show how an account of reasons of respect along the lines suggested here can explain why reasons of respect play a special role in morality, and particularly in its universal part. They also show how the universal meshes with the socially dependent, how the doctrine of respect can be both universal and general in application in its abstract formulation, while being culturally dependent and socially relative in some of its, especially its symbolic, manifestations.

INDEX